People are talking about...

"Some people browse for God in giant tomes and intimidating libraries; others choose the route of rummaging in humble nooks and crannies. Sr. Melannie Svoboda does both—she browses through spiritual giants such as St. Gregory of Nyssa, Evelyn Underhill, and John Henry Newman; she rummages among dishes and squash and snapdragons in search of a loving God. And she shares her finds with us. A nourishing read."

†Robert F. Morneau
Auxiliary Bishop of Green Bay

"This book by popular author Sr. Melannie Svoboda is full of wonderful ways to find God in places we don't expect to discover the Holy One, such as when we feel stressed out or doing the dishes or watching children play. *Rummaging for God* shows us how to turn things inside out and upside down until the face of God peeks out at us among the debris of human life. The depth of the author's faith is apparent in the collection of stories, quotes, and prayers that she uses. This insightful guide to spiritual living provides readers with opportunities to reflect on their own stories and see the sacredness of life everywhere."

Dr. Bridget Mary Meehan
Author of *Praying with Women of the Bible*
and *God Delights in You*

"Sr. Melannie charms the reader with her unique ability to express profound Christian wisdom in simple, credible language. In this new book, one meets challenging truth and finds it surprisingly gentle and enjoyable. Would that all rummaging were so profitable."

Rev. Demetrius Dumm, O.S.B.
St. Vincent Archabbey

"Sister Melannie Svoboda opens each of these readable, practical reflections with a wonderful quotation and closes with a question that draws forth the reader's relevant personal experience. She directs us to find God 'in the stuff of everyday life,' a welcome shift in direction from the old approach of seeking God only in abstract theological concepts."

Kathy Coffey
Author of *Thresholds to Prayer*

"In *Rummaging for God*, Sr. Melannie Svoboda shows how incidents in her life become treasures that put her in touch with God. Everything—from the traffic on her street to the sight of a child meeting a cat for the first time—holds a spiritual insight for her. Those who enjoyed the anecdotes, fresh ways of looking at old ideas, and abundant, rich quotations in Melannie Svoboda's previous books will not be disappointed in this new one."

Mary Kathleen Glavich, SND
Author of *Prayer-Moments for Every Day of the Year*

RUMMAGING
FOR
GOD

*Seeking the Holy
in Every Nook and Cranny*

MELANNIE SVOBODA, SND

A. Melannie Svoboda, SND

TWENTY-THIRD PUBLICATIONS
Mystic, CT 06355

Dedication

To my brother

Paul J. Svoboda

From my earliest days until now
you have been my helper,
accomplice, confidant, and friend—
the faithful companion of all my rummagings.

The Gospel passages contained herein are from the *New Revised Standard Version of the Bible,* copyright © 1989, by the Division of Christian Education of the National Council of Churches of Christ in the U.S.A. All rights reserved.

Second printing 2000

Twenty-Third Publications/Bayard
185 Willow Street
P.O. Box 180
Mystic, CT 06355
(860) 536-2611
(800) 321-0411

ISBN: 0-89622-943-2
Library of Congress Catalog Card Number: 98-61012
Printed in the U.S.A.

Table of Contents

Introduction 1

MEDITATION   **PAGE**

1. Amateurs at Prayer...3
2. The Fear of Wholeness 4
3. The Problem with Love...................................5
4. Love your Enemies 6
5. Making Goodness Attractive 7
6. Behold the Ordinary 8
7. Self-Esteem 9
8. Loving in Little Ways 10
9. Heaven's First Law 11
10. The Annunciation of St. Joseph 12
11. One Wild and Precious Life 13
12. On Doing the Dishes.....................................15
13. Heaven: The Big Reunion 16
14. Laughter 17
15. Stewardship Is Saying, "Nice Kitty"..............18
16. The Difference a Preposition Can Make 19
17. Be Patient with the Seasons 20
18. Criticism 22
19. A Lesson from Fido 23
20. Leaving All 24
21. Keeping Vigil 25
22. The Habit of Doing the Right Thing...............27
23. Gathered Around the Altar 28
24. Is a Better World Possible? 29
25. Thanking God 30

26. Give Yourself a Ticket 32

27. Give Yourself an Ice Cream Cone 33

28. God Always Takes the Initiative 34

29. All About Ashes 35

30. Nearer to Thee, My God 36

31. Butterflies Taste with Their Feet 37

32. God Loves a Cheerful Receiver.........................39

33. Woodward Avenue..40

34. Doors...41

35. Being Jesus for Others......................................42

36. Proverbs 43

37. Getting Off a Dead Horse 44

38. If I Were the Evil Spirit 45

39. The Angelus Bell 47

40. They're Just Like Me 48

41. The Kitten on the Calendar...............................49

42. Making Unpopular Decisions 50

43. Uncle Marty 51

44. Making Others Look Good 53

45. How Dangerous Am I?..54

46. Stay Awake 55

47. Who Is God?..56

48. Thorns Have Roses 57

49. Kissing the Earth with Our Feet 58

50. Religion: Theory or Love Affair? 60

51. Difficult People...61

52. The One-Inch Picture Frame.............................62

53. Children 63

54. Serenity 64

55. Pencil Marks on a Door Frame..........................65

56. A Choice of Attitude 66

57. The Penance of Inconvenience..........................68

MEDITATION	PAGE

58. Two by Two 69
59. You Don't Have Time to Pray? 70
60. The Huggers and the Hiders 71
61. The Psalms: The Real Thing 72
62. Summer Squash and Snapdragons 73
63. On Trembling 75
64. The Man with the Barrel 76
65. The Delight of Children's Proverbs............................77
66. Jesus at the Intersection............................78
67. The Magic of Kevin Kaplowitz 79
68. And Jesus Wept 80
69. The Fragility of an Ego 82
70. Encouraging Words 83
71. Calls in the Evening............................84
72. Three Pigeons in a Crosswalk............................86
73. Why Do We Do Penance? 87
74. The Marching Band 88
75. The Disciples of Jesus 89
76. The Hard Work of Faith............................90
77. Manners............................91
78. The White-Haired Army of Believers 92
79. Spilled Milk............................94
80. Meeting the Real Jesus............................95
81. Creativity: Faith's Dancing Partner 96
82. On Stories 97
83. Work: A Worthwhile Investment............................98
84. Sister Mary David 100
85. You Needed Me 101
86. The Women in My Kitchen 102
87. Thou Shalt Lighten Up............................103
88. Sacred Ambiguity 105
89. Taking Time to Really See............................106

90. Asking Jesus for Help 107

91. Have I Been Good to You Today? 108

92. Seeking God 109

93. Irish Wisdom..111

94. Excellence 112

95. Sorrow and Loss 113

96. Jesus and Touch 114

97. Praying Mantras 115

98. Life Is a Book 116

99. Whose Side Are You On? 118

100. The Ache of Unfulfillment 119

Bibliography 121

Index of Topics..123

RUMMAGING FOR GOD

Introduction

A few years back I came across an article by Dennis Hamm, SJ, entitled "Rummaging for God" (*America*, May 14, 1994). In it, Hamm explains his unique title in these words: "'Rummaging for God' is an expression that suggests going through a drawer full of stuff, feeling around, looking for something that you are sure must be there somewhere." I liked that. When I started writing this book, I recalled Hamm's article and thought, "What a perfect title for this book!" I asked Fr. Hamm if I could use it, and he graciously said yes. I am very grateful.

This is a book about rummaging—rummaging for God in the stuff of our everyday life. It is about rummaging in the places we ordinarily expect to find God—in prayer, at Mass, in Scripture, in love and friendship. But it is also about rummaging for God in places we don't ordinarily expect to find God: while washing dishes, waiting for a traffic light to change, reading the comics, watching children play, feeling stressed out, making dumplings, encountering a trio of pigeons, sitting with a loved one who is dying.

The word "rummage" is a perfect word to describe how we are meant to look for God. First, the word denotes a search that is thorough, not superficial. When we rummage for God, we don't say, "Well, I don't see God right now, so I guess God's not here," and walk away. No, we look hard for God. We lift things up, we crawl underneath them, we turn things upside down and inside out if necessary. Rummaging also implies that we take time to look. It means we look again and again if necessary—even where we have already looked before.

1

The word rummage also implies a certain messiness. And doesn't that describe how life is experienced by us most of the time: messily? Life seldom comes in neat little packages or straight rows. It doesn't come in alphabetical order or logical sequence. No, life often comes to us mixed up, tangled, topsy-turvy. The question is, are we willing to keep rummaging for God even when our lives are in disarray?

When we rummage for things, we get into every nook and cranny. Similarly, when we rummage for God we get into every nook and cranny of our lives—not just the so-called pretty or holy parts. This means we search for God everywhere: in our goodness, joys, and accomplishments as well as our sin, sorrows, and failures.

There's another reason why the word rummage is a good one to describe our search for God. When we rummage, we never know when we're going to find a real treasure. We have all heard stories of people who got lucky at a rummage sale—for example, the man who bought an old picture frame for a couple of dollars only to discover he had really bought a valuable painting worth thousands. Or the woman who bought a small vase for fifty cents only to learn it was worth $25,000. When we rummage for God, we never know when we're going to find a treasure, when we're going to strike it rich.

This book contains one hundred rummagings, that is, one hundred short meditations that grew out of my own searchings for God. But the meditations are not meant to stop with me; they are meant to encourage your own rummaging. To facilitate this, each meditation concludes with a question or two to invite your personal dialogue with the text. In addition, there is a short prayer at the end of each rummaging that grows out of the particular meditation, a line to carry with you as you go about your day. The book can be used for private prayer and reflection as well as for group sharing. And finally, this book also includes an index of topics covered in the various meditations.

What is my hope for this book? It is a simple one: that it may encourage you to continue to search for and discover God in the stuff of your everyday life. For I truly believe, as you may too, that no matter where life takes us, God is already there.

Happy rummaging!

1. Amateurs at Prayer

The ark was built by amateurs, and the Titanic by the experts.
Don't wait for the experts. —Murray Cohen

When we want to learn more about prayer, we are quick to consult the experts in prayer—people like Thomas Aquinas, Teresa of Avila, Francis of Assisi, Julian of Norwich, Ignatius of Loyola, as well as our favorite contemporary spiritual writers. It is true that these so-called experts on prayer can be helpful by providing us with new insights into prayer or new methods of prayer. But we must never assume that only the experts really know how to pray or that, somehow, we must be an expert before we can pray. For the truth is, when it comes to prayer, it's okay to be an amateur. In fact, in some cases, it is even better to be an amateur than a pro.

Jesus told a parable that illustrates this truth: the parable of the Pharisee and the publican, that is, the tax collector (Luke 18:9–14). Most of us know how the story goes. One day a Pharisee struts into the temple to pray. He is the expert on prayer, the professional prayer, if you will. He begins his prayer by thanking God that he is not like the rest of humanity—greedy, dishonest, adulterous—and that he is not like that miserable tax collector standing back there. Then the Pharisee rattles off a list of all the things he has done for God: he has prayed, fasted, and even given alms.

In contrast, we have the publican. He is the amateur at prayer. He stays in the rear of the temple, bows his head, beats his breast, and murmurs: "O God, be merciful to me, a sinner." Jesus declares that it was the publican who offered the finest prayer. It was the amateur who showed up the pro!

Sometimes we can get all bent out of shape over our prayer and think things like this: "I don't know how to pray...my prayer is dumb...everyone else is praying better than I am...if only I were a mystic!" When tempted to think such things, we should recall that humble publican beating his breast in the rear of the temple. And we should remember that God loves to hear our prayer—no matter how simple, awkward, or ordinary it is. Because God loves us, even if we are only amateurs at prayer.

Have I ever acted as if I were an expert at prayer? Do I really believe God loves my prayer no matter how much of an amateur I may be?

✧ God, be merciful to me, a sinner!

2. The Fear of Wholeness

Nothing is more frightening than to be divested of a crutch.

—*James Baldwin*

One of the greatest challenges for people after a long illness is being well again. Those who have been sick for any length of time can, in a way, get used to being sick. They can get used to being in their pajamas, to sleeping most of the day, to thinking only of themselves, to having everyone else wait on them. Once they are well again, it can be difficult to adjust to getting dressed in the morning, to staying up all day, to thinking of others, to doing things for themselves.

Some individuals are actually frightened by the prospect of restored health, by this divestment of their crutch. Or, perhaps more accurately, they are frightened by the responsibilities that this divestment can bring. When they were sick, for example, others did their dishes for them. But now that they are well, others are expecting them not only to do their own dishes, but also to go to work, to run to the grocery store, and to rinse out the tub, for heaven's sake!

A similar dynamic operates on the spiritual level. If we have been spiritually sick for any length of time, we may find the prospect of spiritual health frightening. For we instinctively know that spiritual health, like all gifts from God, brings with it certain responsibilities. When Jesus cures people, for example, he often says to them, "Go home." Perhaps he is really saying this: go back to your town, back to your family, and assume those responsibilities that your illness may have temporarily excused you from. In other words, when Jesus restores health to people, he inserts them back into their everyday world, for it is precisely there that they are to use their newly restored health to serve others.

Have I ever been divested of a crutch? If so, what was the crutch and what was that experience like for me? How am I using my gift of spiritual health to serve others?

✧ Jesus, may I not fear to use my gifts in the service of others today.

3. The Problem with Love

If we love and desire to give ourselves to God, we are bound to give ourselves to the whole world. —Evelyn Underhill

Dear Jesus,

The problem with the kind of love you ask of us is this: it is too specific. It is too concrete. It is too time consuming. We want to love generally, to say, "I love everyone!" But you ask us to love particularly, to say, "I love *you*!" You want us to love this next-door neighbor who plays music too loudly and whose lawn is littered; this friend who has become something of a nuisance lately; this student who is lazy and disrespectful; this son who has brought shame to our family.

We prefer to love quickly, to get it over with so we can get back to things more interesting and more important. But you call us to love unhurriedly, patiently, painstakingly. You ask us, "What is more interesting and more important than love?" We want to love in dramatic ways, with wide and sweeping movements, in laying-down-your-life-for-others kinds of ways. But, most often, you call us to love in ordinary ways, with small and simple gestures, in doing-a-little-favor-for-someone-else kinds of ways.

We wish to forgive only once. You ask us to forgive seven times seventy times. We say, "But...." You say, "No buts."

We wish to love over there, not till then, and only that. But you ask us to love here and now and this. We prefer to love with our lips, but you ask us to love also with our eyes, our ears, our hands, our hearts. We want to send a check, but you ask us to walk over there ourselves. We want to wait until tomorrow, but you ask us to love today. We want to put restrictions on our love, but you ask that our love know no bounds.

The problem with the kind of love you ask of us, Jesus, is this: it accepts no excuses. But, thankfully, this is not only the kind of love you *ask* of us, it is the kind of love you *give* to us. The kind of love you make possible in us.

How specific and concrete is my love for others?

✧ Jesus, give me your love so that I, in turn, may love others as you love me.

4. Love Your Enemies

*But I say to you, love your enemies, and pray for those
who persecute you. —Matthew 5:44*

Most people would agree that the most difficult command Jesus gave us is the one cited above: "Love your enemies, and pray for those who persecute you." Such a directive goes against everything inside of us. Our natural tendency is to hate our enemies and to curse those who persecute us: "Take that, you enemy!" And yet Jesus tells us to love our enemies! How can this be?

On our own, it cannot be. Left to ourselves, the command is impossible to execute. It is only made possible through the power of God's holy Spirit. Notice though, Jesus does not say we must like our enemies. He does not say we must approve of their behavior or beliefs. After all, Jesus himself had some pretty strong words for the scribes and Pharisees, leaving no doubt that he strongly opposed their beliefs and behavior. But Jesus tells us we must love our enemies which, in essence, means we must wish them no harm, we must care about them, we must be willing to sacrifice for them, and we must forgive them.

I am reminded of a story about two little third-grade boys, Nicky and Danny, who were caught fighting on the playground one day. Their teacher intervened and scolded them. That afternoon in class she talked about the importance of love and forgiveness, aiming her remarks directly at the two boys. The next day, the boys' behavior improved on the playground. But a few days later, the teacher found this note in Nicky's workbook: "Dear Nicky, I hate you! Love,

Danny." Even though Danny was still at odds with Nicky, he nevertheless called him "dear" and signed his name with a "love." Maybe there is a lesson in that for us adults!

How well am I living these challenging words of Jesus: "Love your enemies, and pray for those who persecute you"?

✧ Jesus, give me your strength that I may love everyone today—even those whom I may not like.

5. Making Goodness Attractive

A saint is someone who makes goodness attractive.
—Laurence Housman

There are many definitions of the word saint. There is the standard dictionary definition: "A saint is a person recognized for holiness." Then there is the famous nineteenth-century definition: "A saint is a sinner, revised and edited." And finally, there is the somewhat whimsical definition I saw recently: "A saint is someone the sun shines through."

But of all the definitions I have come across, I tend to like this one best: "A saint is someone who makes goodness attractive." Unfortunately, there are some saints who do not make goodness attractive. In fact, they make goodness repugnant or even laughable. I am referring to those saints who did some pretty strange and silly things in the name of holiness; for example, refusing to take a bath, ever!, whipping their bodies until they bled, or living on top of a post for years. If this is goodness and holiness, we might say, we want no part of it!

Fortunately, we have a whole host of saints who do make goodness attractive. They are the ones who devoted their whole lives to caring for others, for God's poor ones—and who did so with great joy. Or the ones who retained their sense of humor even amid terrible persecution or torture. Or the ones whose lives were a living testimony to God's goodness, power, and love.

Though few of us will ever be canonized saints, we are all called to holiness. This means we too share in the task of making goodness attractive. How do we do this? In many ways: by radiating joy, by making choices based on our convictions and not on the latest opinion poll, by being approachable, by being a person of hope, by trusting in God's power at work in us, by looking for the good in others, and by hanging on to our sense of humor.

Who in my life continues to make goodness attractive for me? How do they do this?

✧ God, help me to make goodness attractive today, even in little ways.

6. Behold the Ordinary

Little minds are interested in the extraordinary, great minds in the commonplace. —Elbert Hubbard

I was sitting in a park one day reading a book. Suddenly a young man arrived carrying his little son who was about a year and a half old. When the little boy caught sight of the wide expanse of green grass, he could hardly contain himself. He started jumping up and down in his father's arms trying to get down. Finally his father stood him on the grass. The little boy jumped up and down a few times and laughed. Then he squatted down and began to touch the grass, running his hands back and forth, back and forth, delighting in the feel. He patted the grass a few times and then began pulling it, each time proudly showing his father the few blades he had managed to grab.

As I watched them, I was struck by the little boy's fascination with the grass; but more than that, I was struck by the father's. For he too began running his hands back and forth across the grass, delighting in the feel. He too was examining the grass closely, smelling it, and gazing in wonder at its expansiveness. I thought to myself: it is as if this young father is experiencing grass for the first time—as if he is suddenly realizing what an extraordinary thing ordinary grass really is! And it took his little son to teach him.

We live in a world that touts the extraordinary to such an extent, we can easily become oblivious to the ordinary wonders all around us: a blade of grass, a puddle of water, the song of a robin, the smell of an orange, the feel of a sharp thorn, the lick of a puppy. How much we all need individuals in our lives who call our attention to these miracles of the commonplace.

Jesus was such a person. After all, one of the words he used over and over again was: behold!

Who in my life helps me to behold the miracles of the commonplace? How am I performing this service for others?

✧ Jesus, help me to behold the ordinary miracles in my life today.

7. Self-Esteem

Nobody can make you feel inferior without your consent.
—*Eleanor Roosevelt*

I have been to only two hockey games in my entire life—one last year and one last week. Both times I watched the Windsor Spitfires skate to victory over the opposing teams. But there was one noticeable contrast between the two games. Last year there were very few fights during the game; just your periodic shoving, tripping, and punching that (they tell me) is expected in a hockey game. But last week there were more than a few scuffles. In fact, the entire game was riddled with fights. In the first minute of play, for example, the fighting got so bad that several players were thrown out of the game. (Now, you know the fighting is serious when that happens in a hockey game. Hockey officials are notorious for tolerating most forms of fighting. Anything short of decapitation gets a two-minute penalty for "roughing.")

On the way home (we left early) I kept wondering, "Why was the second game so much more violent?" I tried to come up with some reason for this increase in brutality. My friend gave me the key when he remarked, "Both of those teams are doing poorly this year. They are in last and second-to-last place in the league."

That is it, I thought. Last year both teams were doing very well. They were in first and second place in the league. But this year they are in the cellar—or on the first step going up from the cellar. Why so much fighting this year? The guys are frustrated. They are mad. They are disheartened. They are embarrassed. In short, they have little, if any, self-esteem.

The experience brought me to this conclusion: when one's self-esteem is low, everyone else begins to look like a punching bag. On the other hand, when people feel good about who they are, they do not feel the need to slap other people around. The big question is, how do we help build self-esteem in people? Comedian Eddie Cantor gave us one way. He said, "When I see the 'Ten Most Wanted Lists' in the post office, I always have this thought: if we had made them feel wanted earlier, they wouldn't be wanted now." A good question to ask myself regularly is this: how do I help to make other people feel wanted?

What are some specific ways I can help build self-esteem in the individuals I meet today?

✧ Jesus, help me to make others feel wanted today.

8. Loving in Little Ways

Romance is about little things. —Gregory Godeck

There is an old romantic song entitled, "Have I Told You Lately that I Love You?" Recently I heard Mort Crimm, a Detroit newsman, tell this poignant story about that song. When he was a young boy, he used to hear his parents singing that song to each other. They usually did this only when they did not think he was around. Many years later his father lay dying in the hospital. When he got to the room where his father was, he saw his mother sitting next to his father's bed. She was holding his hand, stroking his head gently, and singing softly through her tears, "Have I told you lately that I love you?"

"Romance is about little things." Yes, it is. It is about brushing the snow off her car, making his favorite dessert, saying "thank you," watching the kids for the day, fixing the toaster, giving a hug for no special reason, saying "I'm sorry."

The spiritual life is about little things, too. It's about getting up fifteen minutes earlier to pray. It's about subscribing to a religious magazine. It's about taking some blueberries to the elderly couple across the street. It's about volunteering for a parish ministry. It's about trying to be more patient with the kids.

When we die, we might find ourselves asking Jesus, "Have I told you lately that I love you?" And hopefully, we just might hear Jesus say to us, "Not only have you *told* me. You *showed* me in a million little ways your whole life long!"

What are some of the little ways I show my love to others and to God?

✧ Jesus, have I told you lately that I love you?

9. Heaven's First Law

Order is not heaven's first law. Generativity is.
—Melannie Svoboda, SND

There was a sign in the cafeteria at my elementary school that said, "Order is heaven's first law." It was an attempt, I assume, to get the workers to put the knives and spoons back into the proper drawers. But if someone were to ask me what I think heaven's first law is, I would say: "Generativity." Definitely. I must admit, I used to say that love was heaven's first law. But the word "love" is so abstract and so overused, I shy away from it now. Besides, we human beings do some pretty awful and outrageous things in the name of love. No, the better word here is generativity, which means "the giving of life."

There is clear scriptural evidence to support this view. After all, when we first meet God in the opening pages of the Bible, what is God doing? God is generating things. In fact, God is shown generating everything—sun, moon, stars, oceans, amoebas, toads, willow trees, armadillos (not necessarily in that order) and (of course) human beings. Then God commands all creatures to share in this generativity, saying: "Increase and multiply," which basically means "Generate life!"

And we generate life in more ways than simply having babies.

In the gospels, we see that generativity was Jesus' top priority, too. Everywhere he went, Jesus generated life. He did this not by having children of his own, but by doing other equally vital tasks: curing the sick, feeding the hungry, enlightening the ignorant, calming the fearful, counseling the confused, embracing the outcast. Jesus' command, "Love one another" really means, "Give life to one another." Be generators!

Whenever I hear the word "generator," I think of something Norm Dickson, a Jesuit friend of mine, told me once. Several years ago he was stationed in East Africa. Living in a remote area, he and his companions were dependent upon a generator for all their electrical power. He told me he grew to love the sound of that generator in the evening after supper, the ever-present, steady hum. "It's hard to explain why," he said. "But the hum of the generator was a real comfort for me. It was so constant, so steady."

God is our divine generator, the one who gives us life, feeds us, enlightens us, heals us, and calms our fears. God is the ever-present, steady hum of our lives calling us to generativity.

Is generativity a top priority in my life? If not, what is? If so, what are some of the ways I am generating life?

✧   God of generativity, help me to generate life in the people I meet today.

10. The Annunciation of St. Joseph

What gives my life meaning is struggle and knowing that God is present in struggle. —Ignacio Castuera

Most of us are familiar with the Annunciation, that time when the angel Gabriel appears to Mary and asks her to become the Mother of God. But did we ever stop to think that Joseph, in his own way, had an annunciation experience, too?

Joseph, Scripture tells us, was the young carpenter from Nazareth who was engaged to Mary. Before they came to live together, however, Mary got pregnant. Both Mary and Joseph knew that Joseph was not the father of the child. What anguish this must have caused Joseph! The young woman he loved, trusted, and was engaged to was pregnant by another man. What should he do? Should he have Mary stoned, as was his right according to the law? For some reason, Joseph could not bring himself to do that. Instead, he decided to divorce Mary quietly.

It is at this point in the story that Joseph has his annunciation. An angel comes to him in the middle of the night as he is tossing and turning in his bed, and tells him to take Mary as his wife, "For it is through the Holy Spirit that this child has been conceived in her" (Matthew 1:20). Now Joseph did not have to do as the angel directed. He could have said, "Yeah, tell me another one!" Or, "I believe you, Mr. Angel, but I am not the guy for the job! Sorry!" But, no, Joseph says "yes" to the angel and to God with just as much faith, just as much courage, and just as much love as Mary did.

We should not imagine that Joseph had an easy life, or that his choices were automatic. No, like us, Joseph experienced anguish and hardship, indecision, and sleepless nights. But, unlike us at times, he held firm to the conviction that somehow God was present in his struggles. At Joseph's annunciation, God called him to trust God, to have courage, and to love with all his heart. We who share Joseph's struggles also share his call.

Do I ever experience anguish and sleepless nights like Joseph? If so, to whom do I turn during such times?

✧ Joseph, you who are so much like me, help me to be more like you!

11. One Wild and Precious Life

> *Tell me, what is it you plan to do with your one wild and precious life? —Mary Oliver*

I was touring Arches National Park in Utah with some friends. Everywhere we looked we saw incredible rock formations: graceful arches, soaring spires, towering pinnacles, each one clamoring for our attention, each one eliciting our awe. After several hours we were literally exhausted by the veritable onslaught of beauty. As we were driving out of the park, one of my friends gestured toward a huge rock by the side of the road, a seemingly "ordinary" one compared to some of the others, but, in truth, a highly extraordinary one. He said, "Now if that rock were suddenly lifted up and transported to central Ohio, people would come from miles around just to see it. But here, among so many other incredible rocks, it barely gets noticed."

My friend was right. His remark led me to wonder: do we ever really appreciate things in a clump, so to speak, or can we only appreciate them one at a time? Is too much of a good thing just too much for us? Is taking things for granted our human way of coping with too much beauty, too much truth, too much love?

One of my favorite poems by Emily Dickinson begins with this line: "Tell all the truth, but tell it slant." Dickinson is not advocating lying. She goes on to explain why she thinks we should tell the truth "slant": because the straight truth is "too bright for our infirm eyes." The whole truth would blind us.

The truth is, the gift of life is marvelous, incredible. "Why me?" is a question we should ask every morning when we crawl out of bed, not out of self-pity, but out of profound gratitude for the gift of another day. A second question should be addressed to the face we meet in the mirror each morning: "Tell me, what is it you plan to do—today—with your one wild and precious life?"

Is there a precious something or someone in my life that I am taking for granted? What do I plan to do today with my one wild and precious life?

✧ Loving God, why me? Thank you! Thank you!

12. On Doing the Dishes

*The best time for planning a book is while you're
doing the dishes. —Agatha Christie*

I am going to write a sentence I thought I would never write. Here
it goes: "Deep down, I like doing the dishes." Now, if my mother
reads that sentence, she won't believe it. After all, for years she had
to remind, summon, beseech, beg, cajole, order, and compel me to
do the dishes. If my sister reads that sentence, she won't believe it
either. For she too spent considerable time in her youth yelling at me
to GET OVER HERE THIS INSTANT AND HELP ME WITH THESE
DISHES...OR ELSE! What accounts for my radical change of heart?

For one thing, I am now old enough to appreciate what Agatha
Christie said, "The best time for planning a book is while you're
doing the dishes." Only I would expand it: "The best time for doing
a lot of things is while you're doing the dishes." It's a good time to
talk with someone, especially if one of you is washing and the other
one is drying. Doing dishes together is a great way to get to know
people. During my first years in the convent, for example, some of
my best friendships were forged at the kitchen sink while I was slosh-
ing around and slinging pots and pans with my fellow novices. In
more recent years, when I mooch a meal off my parents, I enjoy
standing at the kitchen sink with my mother after supper, chatting
about little things, while doing those dishes that don't fit into the
dishwasher or those you cannot trust Matilda with. (Matilda is my
mother's dishwasher.) Doing dishes with Mom is, for me, a sacred
moment, a kind of religious ritual.

If you are doing the dishes alone, it is a good time to think. About
what? About anything really. The very act of putting your hands in
warm sudsy water can actually stimulate thinking—especially the
slow, rambling, take-all-the-time-you-need kind of thinking. Doing
dishes is also a wonderful time to pray. It is a good time to recall some
of the key events of the day where you may have felt God's presence
and to say, "Thank you, God." Or those moments when you may have
felt God's apparent absence, and to ask, "Where were you, God?"
Doing dishes is also a good time to plan your tomorrow, or at least to
ask God to help you come up with a few preliminary sketches.

Pope John XXIII used to say, "Every day is a good day." We can add, every routine task—like doing the dishes, running the vacuum, carrying out the garbage, washing the car—is a good time to talk to God.

Do I ever talk to God when I'm performing routine tasks? What are some of the everyday religious rituals in my own life?

✧ God, help me to pause during my busy day to say "thank you" or "where are you?"

13. Heaven: The Big Reunion

> *Those who live in the Lord never see each other*
> *for the last time. —German proverb*

Death has been called "that final farewell." And in some ways, it is. For when we die, we say farewell to everything we know on this earth: people, places, the sun, moon, sky, oceans, apple trees, cream puffs, baboons—you name it. Death is even a farewell to our own body, it seems. Yes, death is a goodbye: *but* (and that "but" is an important one!) for those of us who are Christians, death is not a final goodbye. It is a temporary one, especially when it comes to the people we know and love. For, as the German proverb says, "Those who live in the Lord never see each other for the last time."

Years ago I saw an ancient painting somewhere that depicted what heaven was going to be like. The artist showed dozens of people meeting and embracing one another. That's all. Just a bunch of people meeting and embracing. Studying the picture, I remember thinking, "Why, it looks like some cosmic family reunion!" Precisely.

For if heaven is about anything at all, it is about reunion. It is about being joined again with those we love. If it is not about that, then, quite frankly, I cannot get too excited about going there. Years ago, an elderly sister in her nineties confided to me how much she still missed her parents—and they had been dead for over sixty years! She said to me, "When I get to heaven and meet Jesus, I'll say something like, 'Hi, Jesus. It's nice to meet you. Now where's Mom and Dad?'" It was not that this sister wasn't looking forward to finally meeting her

Lord and savior; it was that she knew one of the reasons she clung so tenaciously to her belief in Jesus was because he promised reunion with our loved ones after death. She believed so strongly in Jesus' resurrection because it included the resurrection of all of us.

Our belief in the resurrection, in that final reunion, does not take away the intense pain we can feel when a loved one dies. Nor will it necessarily remove all the fears we may have concerning our own death. But our belief in the resurrection can and often does make our pain more bearable, our fears less daunting. For at death, when we bid our loved ones "goodbye," we're really saying this: "Goodbye for now. But I'll see you again, at the big reunion!"

How strong is my faith in Jesus' resurrection? in my own resurrection? in that of my loved ones?

✧ Jesus, strengthen my belief in heaven as the big reunion.

14. Laughter

Of all days, the day on which one has not laughed is the one most surely wasted. —Sebastian-Roch Nicolas Chamfort

I agree with Chamfort's words. You probably do too. Regular laughter is essential for our physical and spiritual well-being. A day without laughter is, at the very least, an anemic one. But sometimes we live such busy and fretful lives that we forget to make time for laughter. The following humorous thoughts are meant to make you laugh—or at least smile.

• Always borrow from pessimists: they never expect anything back anyway.

• Sign seen in a veterinarian's office: The doctor is in. Sit. Stay.

• Middle age is when your knees buckle and your belt doesn't.

• The *Washington Post* asked its readers to send in ideas for useless products. The list included these: silicone thigh implants, a fire alarm with snooze bar, and an inflatable dartboard.

• When weeding, the best way to make sure you're removing

a weed and not a valuable plant is to pull on it. If it comes out of the ground easily, it's a valuable plant.

- Sign over the scale in a doctor's office: Pretend it's your I.Q.
- After substituting in a fourth grade class for six weeks, a teacher received a large thank-you card from the kids saying in big letters: "In such a short time, you taught us all you know!"
- Why is there so much month left at the end of the money?
- Definition of a born loser: someone who gets a paper cut from a get-well card.
- Before I got married I had six theories about bringing up children. Now I have six children and no theories.

Do I laugh on a regular basis? If not, what can I do about it?

✣ God, help me to bring laughter to others today.

15. Stewardship Is Saying, "Nice Kitty"

*If the earth does grow inhospitable toward human presence,
it is primarily because we have lost our sense of courtesy
toward the earth and its inhabitants. —Thomas Berry*

I was there that day when little Missy met Friskers, her first cat. When Missy toddled into the room with her mother and spotted Friskers sitting there on the living room chair, she ran toward him excitedly, reached out to him, and grabbed him by the ear. "No, Missy!" her mother cried out. "Don't hurt the kitty!" Needless to say, Friskers was not exactly eager to make Missy's acquaintance after having his ear yanked. He would have darted away, no doubt, except that Missy's mother, realizing there was a lesson to be taught here, picked him up and held him in front of her little girl. Then she said, "Pet the kitty nicely, Missy—like this," and she stroked the cat a few times saying: "Nice kitty…nice kitty." Missy caught on right away. She gently patted Friskers on top of the head a couple of times and said, "Nice kitty…nice kitty." As soon as Missy's mother let Friskers go, he shot out of the room and wasn't seen for the rest of the afternoon.

Afterwards, I thought: Missy had just received a lesson in stewardship. It was not her first one, mind you, for I had heard her mother say things before like, "Nice flower…nice doggie…nice baby." The first step in stewardship is realizing that things are nice; consequently, we must do them no harm. I imagine this was the same lesson God had to teach Adam and Eve in the garden of Eden. Maybe the first time Adam and Eve saw a lion, they ran up to it excitedly and began pulling its mane or yanking its tail. And God had to say, "Now Adam, now Eve, pet the lion nicely, like this: Nice kitty…nice kitty."

If the first lesson in stewardship is, "Do no harm," then the second one is this: "Watch over. Take care of. Tend." Stewardship goes beyond a mere "let live" attitude and asks, "Can I do anything to help?"

Stewardship says, "Nice kitty…nice pine tree…nice river…nice eagle…nice whale…nice people." In short, nice world!

How am I practicing stewardship in my daily life?

✧ God, help me to show my gratitude for this world by treating everything and everyone nicely today, and by asking, "Is there anything I can do to help you?"

16. The Difference a Preposition Can Make

The kingdom of God is among you. —Luke 17:21

When I was studying the English language many years ago, our instructor made a point I never forgot. She said one of the most important parts of speech in any language are the prepositions. At first I didn't want to believe her. After all, I thought, aren't nouns and verbs like "democracy" and "cherish" much more important than a lowly "in" or "to" or "by"? When she explained why, it made sense to me.

Prepositions indicate relationships. They connect things to one another. There's a big difference, for example, between saying "The man is *on* the elephant" and "The man is *in* the elephant"—especially if you are the man. Or between saying "Esther ran *to* Fred" and "Esther ran *from* Fred" and "Esther ran *into* Fred." Each preposition paints a very different picture of Esther's relationship to Fred. The first could mean she loves Fred; the second, she hates him; the third, she just happened to meet him on the street. Yes, prepositions are important.

This point is demonstrated in a line from the Gospel of Luke. One day, a group of Pharisees asks Jesus, "When is the kingdom of God coming?" Jesus tells them that the kingdom of God isn't coming. "For, in fact, the kingdom of God is among you" (Luke 17:21).

Some translations use a different preposition. They say, "The kingdom of God is within you." But current scholarship prefers "among." What is the difference? If the kingdom of God is within, that means it is inside of me and inside of you. Each of us, therefore, is a walking little kingdom, so to speak. But the preposition "among" adds a dimension that "within" misses. It implies that the kingdom is not something each of us holds separately. It is something we share together. The kingdom is not something that happens to me in isolation from you. It is something that happens between us.

The bottom line is this: the preposition "among" reminds us that Jesus calls us not as isolated individuals, but as a family, as friends— as individuals connected to other individuals. Furthermore, we do not hasten the coming of the kingdom solely by loving Jesus, but also by loving our brothers and sisters in him.

Have I ever experienced Jesus' words, "The kingdom of God is among you?" If so, when, where, and how?

✧ Jesus, let me be more aware of your words today: "The kingdom of God is among you."

17. Be Patient with the Seasons

There are winters and summers, it cannot be all the year round the same. —Mother Janet Erskine Stuart

Janet Erskine Stuart, a native of England, was a Religious of the Sacred Heart who lived from 1857 to 1914. A renowned educator as well as a leader for her congregation, Stuart wrote many letters to her sisters and friends throughout her life. *The Inward Life* is a collection of some of those letters. In one of them she is writing to a friend who is experiencing turmoil after making what had been a very peaceful and consoling retreat. Stuart says, "In the leisure of retreat, things are much simpler than in the stress of active life." Probably many of us have experienced the truth of these words even if we have never made a formal retreat. It is easy, for example, to make a good resolution during Mass only to break it before you are even out of the parking lot!

Stuart goes on to say, "There are winters and summers, it cannot be all the year round the same; there would be no fruit if it were so." How true! If it were perpetually summer, we would have no apples. An apple tree needs all four seasons to produce good fruit. If this is true on the physical level, why, then, do we expect things to be different on the spiritual level? Why do we wish for or even demand perpetual summers for our souls? Don't we trust that growth is occurring in our spiritual lives even when we are experiencing the winter of darkness and despair?

Being a writer helps me to believe this great truth a little more easily. There are some writing days when the words and ideas come gushing out, and I cannot type fast enough. But then there are days when I cannot seem to write even one decent sentence, days when all ideas seem to have jumped ship. I used to get depressed when this happened, or worse yet, felt fearful or guilty. But over the years I have learned to be more patient with the ebb and flow of writing, to accept these so-called "bad" writing days as one of the seasons in the writing process.

Stuart concludes with these words of advice to her friend, "You must be patient with the seasons and do the little you can do." Some days we are able to do a lot. We work well, we pray well, we love well. Thank God! But on some days, we must be patient with doing the little we can do, and trust that God is bringing forth fruit even if we cannot see any buds yet.

Do I experience different seasons in my spiritual life? If so, what helps me to get through the winters?

✧ God, you are the one who brings forth spiritual fruit in my life. Knowing this, I will be more patient with the winters of my soul.

18. Criticism

The trouble with most of us is that we would rather be ruined by praise than saved by criticism. —Norman Vincent Peale

Years ago, a friend of our family told us this story. One day, he was driving his old Ford down a long and relatively steep hill when, suddenly, he saw a tire rolling down the hill ahead of him. His first thought was, "Wow! Somebody lost a tire!" but, as the tire rolled off the road and into the ditch, he drove on. He got to the bottom of the hill where he had to stop for a light. That's when another car pulled up along side of him. The driver motioned and pointed frantically to the front of his car. It was only then that he realized the disconcerting truth: the tire that was rolling down the hill was *his* tire!

As a child, I always I liked that story, for it amazed me that a car could actually keep going with only three tires. But now I like the story for another reason. It illustrates how important it is to have other people in our lives who can point out what's wrong with us. In other words, we all need good critics to help us along the way. I say good critics for a reason. A good critic is someone who tells us the truth even if it may hurt, but who does so out of genuine love and concern for us.

I venture to say that few of us enjoy criticism, especially receiving it. Criticism can be embarrassing: it suggests that we may not be as good as we thought we were. It can also be unsettling: we might have to make a change in ourselves. But, as the quote above by Norman Vincent Peale implies, criticism can also be redemptive; it can help fashion us into a better person, a more caring and sensitive one.

Jesus offered criticism. Words such as "beware...love one another...have faith" all imply that his listeners were not bewaring, not loving one another, or not having faith. At the same time, he offered his criticism with a healthy dose of love: "I call you friends," he said on more than one occasion. Jesus had some strong words for the religious leadership of his day, true, but he showed his love for them by forgiving them from the cross.

One of my favorite stories about criticism concerns the poet Carl Sandburg. It seems a playwright asked Sandburg to attend the dress rehearsal of his play so he could critique it. Sandburg did, but he fell asleep during the performance. The playwright was angry: "Don't you know how much I needed your opinion?" he asked. Sandburg replied, "Sleep *is* an opinion."

How well do I give and receive criticism? Have I ever experienced criticism as redemptive?

✧ Jesus, help me to give and receive criticism with love.

19. A Lesson from Fido

> *I have learned more from my dog than from all the*
> *great books I have read. —Gerry Spencer*

Sometimes I envy dogs. I'm speaking of dogs with good homes, mind you. Not the ones pathetically roaming our city streets or the ones chained to barns or doghouses for days on end. No, I envy dogs with good homes, because they have it made. They get fed, petted, walked, and played with every single day—and they do virtually nothing to deserve it. Oh sure, they provide companionship, guard the house while we're gone, fetch the paper, or bark when a stranger comes to the door. But other than that, most dogs do not do an ounce of real work. That is one reason I envy them, but not the primary one.

The primary reason I envy dogs is because they are exceptionally wise. In his book *How to Argue and Win Every Time*, Gerry Spencer puts it this way: "The wisdom of my dog is the product of his inability to conceal his wants." How true that is! When dogs, for example want to go outside, they keep fussing until someone sooner or later lets them outside. When dogs are not feeling well, they do not try to conceal that fact. Instead, they droop their head and go lie down in the corner. When dogs need affection, they ask for it by putting their head on your lap and looking up at you with sad eyes until you give in and pet them. If only we humans were more like Fido. If only we were better at revealing our wants.

One reason, I suspect, that St. Peter appeals to so many people is this: he did not conceal his wants. He did not try to hide his needs. Now, I am not saying St. Peter was a dog, but the fact remains, he always spoke his mind. He always let others know what he was thinking and feeling—even when it got him into trouble. After the miraculous catch of fish, Peter says to Jesus, "Go away from me, Lord, for I am a sinful man!" (Luke 5:8). At the transfiguration, it is Peter who blurts out, "Lord, it is good for us to be here, let us make three dwellings" (Mark 9:5). After the resurrection, Jesus meets with Peter on the seashore and asks him, "Peter do you love me?" And Peter confesses, "Yes, Lord, you know that I love you" (John 21:16). In short, we always know where Peter stands. Even more importantly, Peter knows where Peter stands.

Perhaps that is the real danger here: if we conceal our wants from others, we run the risk of concealing them even from ourselves.

What are some of the ways I let others know my needs and wants?
How sensitive am I to the needs and wants of others?

✧ God, let me share with you today my needs and my wants.

20. Leaving All

To stand on the side of life we must give up our own lives.
—Dorothy Day

One day while Jesus is strolling along the Sea of Galilee, he spots two fisherman, Simon and Andrew, two brothers. Jesus says to them: "Come follow me." At once, the men leave their nets and follow him (Matthew 4:18–22). Later on, Jesus is passing by a customs house and notices Matthew sitting at one of the tables. He says to him: "Follow me." Immediately, Matthew gets up and leaves his stacks of coins on the table and follows Jesus (Luke 5:27–29). The point is clear: discipleship with Jesus always involves a leaving.

But our leaving is never a once-and-for-all thing. When the first disciples left their nets and tax table, they probably thought they had, indeed, left all. Peter says as much when, later on, he reminds Jesus, "We have left all things and followed you" (Luke 18:28). But the apostles soon learned that their initial leaving was only the first of many. It would be followed by deeper, more difficult kinds of leaving. After all, it is one thing to leave one's job and quite another thing to leave one's reputation, one's independence, one's self-confidence, one's control. Yet these are exactly the things that the apostles were asked to leave, especially during the demoralizing passion and death of Jesus, their Lord and friend.

Even after the resurrection and ascension, the apostles still had more to leave behind—most notably, some of their cherished religious beliefs. Peter, for example, like so many other Jews of his day, believed that the Jews held a unique place in God's heart, and that Gentiles, at best, were second-class citizens in God's kingdom. Peter believed this, that is, until God gently and dramatically made it clear to him that salvation is for all, equally, Jew and Gentile alike. The Peter who warmly welcomes the Gentile Cornelius into the church is a far cry from the Peter who left his nets on the shore a few years before. In the final analysis, the hardest things to leave behind are ideas and attitudes, especially if they are part of our religious beliefs.

We might ask, where will all these leavings take us? Perhaps St. Paul gives us the answer when he says of himself: "It is no longer I who live, but it is Christ who lives in me" (Galatians 2:20). We leave behind all that is not of Christ so that we, like Paul, may be transformed into him.

Has my discipleship with Jesus involved any leavings? If so, what did I leave? Is Jesus calling me today to leave behind any ideas or attitudes that are not of him?

✧ Jesus, help me to leave all and follow you.

21. Keeping Vigil

The price of freedom is eternal vigilance.
—*Inscription near the Tomb of the Unknown Soldier*

During the Vietnam war, A.J. Muste stood in front of the White House night after night with a candle, often alone. One rainy night, a reporter stopped by to interview him. He said, "Mr. Muste, do you really think you're going to change the policies of this country by standing out here alone at night with a candle?" Muste replied, "I don't do this to change the country. I do this so the country won't change me."

There can exist in our lives a fundamental tension between our faith and the world in which we live. As Christians we are called to be *in* the world but not *of* the world. People who travel to other lands to evangelize sometimes experience this tension in a unique way. Long before they step into a foreign land, they spend considerable time familiarizing themselves with the country and its people. They study the language, history, and customs. When they finally arrive in the country, they work hard at "fitting in." After all, if they hope to be effective they must identify themselves with the people they want to serve. Part of Jesus' own effectiveness in ministry was his ability to identify with those to whom he ministered. The people saw him as "one of us."

But the people also saw Jesus as someone different from themselves. He was somehow set apart from them. Our faith challenges us to be set apart, too. It calls us to be *not* of the world, that is, to be countercultural. This means we must not adopt those attitudes and practices of our world, our culture, that are contrary to our faith. Like the lone man keeping vigil with his candle, we must be on guard lest out culture change us, that is, lest it lead us to forsake our Christian principles. This is no small task.

How do we prevent ourselves from being swept away by the culture in which we live? We do this in essentially two ways: by knowing our faith and by knowing our culture. How do we get to know our faith better? In a variety of ways: by really listening to the homily each Sunday, by discussing our faith with other believers, by reading religious publications, by attending lectures or parish missions, by praying. Secondly, we must get to know our culture better. This is challenging, for it is never easy to know something we are completely immersed in. Yet periodically, we should step back from our culture and evaluate for ourselves those values our society says are important; for example, freedom, individual rights, consumerism, power, security. To what extent can we buy into these values? To what extent can we not?

The inscription near the Tomb of the Unknown Soldier says, "The price of freedom is eternal vigilance." We could add, so too is the price of living our faith.

What values do I accept in my culture? What values do I reject?

✧ God, keep vigil with me today.

22. The Habit of Doing the Right Thing

A good person is not one who does the right thing, but one who is in the habit of doing the right thing.
—Rabbi Abraham Heschel

Once a friend e-mailed me a list of "Reasons It's Great to be a Guy." Some of the reasons were:

- You can be showered and ready in ten minutes.
- Your phone conversations never last more than thirty seconds.
- You can go on a five-day vacation with only one suitcase.
- Your bathroom lines are eighty percent shorter.
- Three pair of shoes are more than enough.
- Wedding dress, $2000; tuxedo rental, $100.

But there was one reason that caught my attention. It said: "You get extra credit for the slightest act of thoughtfulness." I suspect that women do tend to be more thoughtful than men (why else would this item have appeared on the list?), but that's not the point. The point is: if I am thoughtful only on very rare occasions, I really cannot call myself a thoughtful person. Or, as Heschel says in the quote above, the good person is not one who does the right thing occasionally, but "one who is in the habit of doing the right thing."

When some people hear the word "habit" they automatically think of bad habits—like biting your nails, losing your temper, or leaving your dirty dishes in the sink. Many of us struggle our whole lives trying to rid ourselves of bad habits. But maybe we don't take enough time to acknowledge and appreciate our good habits. After all, a virtue is nothing more than a good habit.

It is wise to take stock of the good habits we have developed over a lifetime, all those right things we habitually do that we may take for granted. Do we get out of bed in the morning even when we don't feel like it? Do we show up for work? Are we basically responsible?

Do we try to pray? Do we go to church regularly? Do we care about others? Do we do things for others? Are we thoughtful? Are we honest? Do we smile a lot? Do we drive safely? Are we polite?

We won't get extra credit for our good habits, it's true, but they can bring us happiness and eventually help lead us to eternal life.

What are some of my good habits that I easily take for granted?

✧ God, give me the habit of doing the right thing today.

23. Gathered Around the Altar

> *The generating principle of our unification is...the single attraction exercised by the same someone.*
> —*Pierre Teilhard de Chardin, SJ*

I was attending Sunday Mass in a church that was built in the round. This layout made it easy for me to notice the people on the other side of church. As Mass began, I found myself staring curiously at the people on the other side of the altar. Catching myself, I said, "Melannie! Stop staring at those people and concentrate on the Mass!" I did concentrate on the liturgy—but only for a few minutes. Then I caught myself staring at the people again. Frustrated with myself, I finally said, "Go ahead! Stare at those people! Maybe God's got a message for you in them." So I gave myself over to my staring.

The first person that caught my attention was a young woman standing with her husband and six children—all boys! The oldest was about eleven; the youngest was still in her arms. I couldn't begin to imagine what her life was like with all those children. I found myself thinking, "How different we are from each other!" I tried to picture what she would be doing after church: cooking dinner, cleaning up the dishes, playing with the kids, refereeing fights, wiping away tears. What a sharp contrast from me, for I planned on being alone this particular Sunday, hunched over my computer, writing. Surely this woman and I had almost nothing in common—she, a young wife and mother, and I, a middle-aged nun.

Then suddenly the thought struck me. No, we did have something in common: this altar! What we had in common far outweighed differences in age or vocation or occupation: our belief in Jesus Christ. In fact, what had brought both of us to that altar was our common need to praise, to ask forgiveness, to beg for help, to receive nourishment. This realization prompted me to look at some of the other people at Mass that day. I saw an elderly African American woman stooped but singing, a tall, lanky teenage boy who seemed more interested in the young girl across the aisle than in what was going on at the altar, a man in an expensive suit, a pretty Oriental woman with long black hair. As different as we all were from each other, we all had one crucial thing in common: our faith. That is what had brought each one of us to the altar that day.

Sometimes the most obvious differences matter the least: gender, age, race, height, occupation. And the least obvious likeness matters the most: our common belief in God.

What do I have in common with individuals who seem very different from me?

✧ Jesus, remind me today what I have in common with those who seem very different from me.

24. Is a Better World Possible?

It's really a wonder that I haven't dropped all my ideals, because they seem so absurd and impossible to carry out. Yet I keep them, because in spite of everything I still believe people are really good at heart. —Anne Frank

These famous words of Anne Frank never cease to amaze me. How could a young Jewish girl, hiding away from the Nazis in a tiny attic, still cling to her belief in the basic goodness of humanity? It is almost beyond comprehension. Our world today, though in some ways improved from Anne Frank's world, is nonetheless still filled with selfishness, greed, violence, and cruelty, making it is almost impossible for us to hang on to our ideals. How much easier it is for us to give in to cynicism.

Rich Heffern, associate editor of *Praying* magazine, says cynicism is the little voice that says, "No better world is possible." We meet cynicism everywhere: in our homes, schools, offices, parishes, and government. For example, when one spouse suggests that the other spouse have a talk with their son, the cynic says, "What's the use?" When the pastor suggests having a parish mission, the cynic responds, "Nobody will come." When the principal suggests a change in a school policy, the cynic says, "It won't make any difference." In short, the cynic believes that nothing we do is going to make this world a better place. So there!

Strictly speaking, you can't be a cynic and be a Christian at the same time. The two are incompatible. For the underlying message of Jesus Christ was precisely this: a better world *is* possible! Isn't this what Jesus meant when he said, "The kingdom of God is among you"? What's more, not only does Jesus assure us that a better world is possible, he tells us exactly what we must do to bring about that better world. He says, "Fear not...repent...have faith...trust in God...behold...love one another...forgive one another...pray always...follow me."

It is tempting to succumb to cynicism. But our faith encourages us to resist that temptation. It invites us instead, with the power of Jesus' spirit, to hope and work for a better world.

Are there any signs that I have succumbed to cynicism? What helps me to hang on to hope?

✧ Jesus, help me to hope and work for a better world today.

25. Thanking God

No one can be grateful and unhappy. —Anthony DeMello, SJ

In her wonderful book, *Undercurrents: A Therapist's Reckoning with Her Own Depression*, Martha Manning describes going to her parents' home for Thanksgiving. She was not looking forward to the visit, because the past year had been hard for nearly every member of her family: a breakup of a marriage, depression, accidents, life-threatening illness, addiction, and the estrangement of one family member.

When the family is seated at the table, her father makes the sign of the cross and says grace. He's all right when he sticks to the "Bless us, O Lord..." part. But when he ventures into the extemporaneous part, the trouble begins. He says, "And thank you for the many ways you have blessed our family this year...." At those words, one of Manning's sisters begins to giggle. Finally she bursts out laughing and says, "Dad, what are you talking about? This is the worst year our family has ever had!" Everyone agrees. Manning's mother tries to say, "Well, at least we're all together." To which someone reminds her that they cannot even be grateful for that, for one of them is not there.

The family sits there arguing with each other about whether they can even pray grace. After all, what can they honestly thank God for? Suddenly, Manning's brother speaks up. He is Mark, a drummer in a rock band, with long hair and black leather pants. Manning says of him: "He's the person who probably logged the least amount of time within a church." But Mark says, "Damn it, I'm grateful. I'm grateful that I survived this year. And I thank God you all did, too." His words silence everyone. For a few minutes they just sit there savoring the wisdom of what he has said. Eventually, they do pray their grace together and enjoy their Thanksgiving dinner.

There are times in our lives when it is hard to say thank you to God. Perhaps we or a loved one are seriously ill. Or we find ourselves in the middle of an unraveling relationship. Or we are struggling with loneliness or depression. Or we are just tired of putting up with our own failures and shortcomings. So we ask, how can we give thanks?

We can if we truly believe that God is present and active in our lives at all times—not just the so-called good times. For our faith tells us that God is at work in sun and darkness, pleasure and pain, harmony and dissonance. We thank God, then, not just because things work out the way we want them to work out. No, we thank God for being a God who, from messiness, brings forth beauty; from absurdity, meaning; and from death, everlasting life.

Do I truly believe that God is present and active in my life at all times? Have I ever experienced God bringing forth beauty from messiness, meaning from absurdity, or life from death?

✥ God, give me a strong sense of your active presence in my life today.

26. Give Yourself a Ticket

Let the one among you who is without sin be the first
to throw a stone at her. —John 8:7

Sgt. Steven Rogers of Nutley, New Jersey, is a very honest cop. One day he spotted a woman struggling with some packages. He pulled over to the side of the street, parked his car, and went to help her. Then, forgetting about his car, he walked to a nearby diner for lunch. While there, he was notified by the dispatcher that someone had reported his car illegally parked. Rogers promptly went outside, moved his car, and wrote himself a seventeen-dollar parking ticket.

"I was thinking about pleading not guilty, but I would have had to cross-examine myself in court," he joked. Then he added, "Besides, my integrity means a lot to me."

It is sometimes easy for us to give tickets to other people, that is, to criticize and judge them: "She's so nosey...he's a real pain...they're both so selfish." But what about ourselves? Are we completely free of the failings we note in others? Do we ever stop and write ourselves a ticket? What kind of a ticket? Maybe a ticket for being crabby, for assuming the worst, for belittling someone, for being ungrateful, or even for being judgmental.

One day the scribes and Pharisees bring to Jesus a woman caught in adultery. (I always wonder, whatever happened to the man? Did he run away? Did they let him go? Or was he a decoy? We'll never know, I suppose.) The men ask Jesus what to do with the woman. They remind him (as if he needed reminding) that the law of Moses says they should stone her. Now, stoning did not mean tossing a few pebbles at the woman. (Take that, you bad lady! Ping!) No, it meant hurling sharp rocks, heaving blunt boulders at her. If you were lucky, you would break a few bones and lacerate the flesh before actually doing her in with a big one to the head.

Jesus has a dilemma. If he says, "Stone her," what does that do to all the love and forgiveness stuff he's been preaching lately? But if he says, "No, let her go," he'll be judged not only "soft on crime," but as setting himself up as better than Moses. Luckily, Jesus finds the perfect "out." He stoops down and begins writing in the dirt with his finger. We don't know what he wrote, but some have conjectured it might have been the sins of the men standing around him. Whatever it was, Jesus then stands up and utters those classic words: "Let the one among you who is without sin be the first to throw a stone at her" (John 8:7). We all know what happens next: one by one, beginning with the eldest, the men walk away.

Charity begins at home. So does the awareness of sin.

Am I judgmental of others? Do I ever write myself a ticket?

✧ Jesus, give me an awareness of my own sin today, coupled with the awareness of your forgiveness.

27. Give Yourself an Ice Cream Cone

If your compassion does not include yourself, it is incomplete.
                                                              —Jack Kornfield

A number of years ago I was driving alone, on my way home from a meeting downtown. It was a sweltering day and I had no air conditioner in the car. I was hot and sweaty. I found myself thinking, "Now, if I had someone in the car, I'd stop and treat her to an ice cream cone." It was a passing thought, nothing more. I kept right on driving—and sweating.

Later, as I reflected on my day, that thought came back to me. "If I had someone in the car...someone in the car...." I suddenly realized that I *did* have someone in the car: myself! Why, in heaven's name didn't I stop and treat myself to an ice cream cone? After all, I'm a person too! (And a pretty nice one, at that.) The incident spoke volumes to me about my lack of self-esteem during that particular period in my life. It was a time when I was doing all kinds of favors for others, but none whatsoever for myself.

One day a scholar of the law says to Jesus: "Teacher, which commandment in the law is the greatest?" Jesus tells him: "You shall love your God with all your heart and soul and mind." Then Jesus adds, "The second is like it: You shall love your neighbor as yourself" (Matthew 22:36–40). "As yourself," Jesus says. Is he really advocating that we treat ourselves with just as much respect and affection as we would our neighbor? Apparently so.

In his book, *After 50: Spiritually Embracing Your Own Wisdom Years*, Robert Wicks tells of a woman who came to him for counseling. He describes how, over time, she went from "being sad, mistrustful, fearful, and rigid to playful and generous." Wick asked her, "How have you done it?" The woman replied, "Simple. I just watched the way you interacted with me and I started treating myself in the same way."

In the previous meditation I suggested we give ourselves a ticket every once in a while. In this one, I'm strongly suggesting we regularly treat ourselves to an ice cream cone!

Do I treat myself with respect and affection? If not, why not? If so, how?

✧ Jesus, keep reminding me today to love my neighbor as myself.

28. God Always Takes the Initiative

Goal of our sighs, remind me
I'm touching on you
—James Torrens, SJ

I went to an all-girls Catholic high school. One of the few negative consequences of that arrangement was this: I had to ask a boy to take me to my own school dances. I know times have changed since then, and today, when it comes to dating, women are taking more initiative. But back then it was highly unusual and (some would say) downright shocking for a girl to ask a boy to a dance. For me personally, it was not just unusual and shocking; it was pure torture.

For weeks I would try to decide who I was going to ask. The ultimate criterion was not looks, not personality, not a convertible. It was this: who is most likely to say yes? Once I decided on that, it would take me days to work up enough courage to actually call the guy and ask him. I was good at coming up with all kinds of reasons not to call the boy at that particular time. I would tell myself, "He's probably not at home…he's watching TV…maybe he's got a cold…he's probably busy that night, anyway…maybe some other girl has already asked him." Finally, when I could procrastinate no longer, I'd drag myself to the phone, pick it up, dial the number, and hold my breath.

What does my teenage trauma have to do with the spiritual life? It's simple. When it comes to our relationship with God, God always takes the initiative. This means we don't have to worry about asking God to the dance; God is already on the phone asking us! John Kavanaugh, SJ, says it well: "As acute and overwhelming as our thirst for God might be, as exhausting and enervating as our journeys to God might seem, the yearning that God has for us and the journey that God has made into our hearts surpasses it all infinitely. Drink it in."

Have I ever experienced God taking the initiative in my life? If so, when and how? Do I really believe that God thirsts for me more than I thirst for God?

✧ God, give me a deep experience of your thirst for me today. Continue to take the initiative in our relationship.

29. All About Ashes

Every Christian truth, gracious and comfortable, has a corresponding obligation, searching and sacrificial.
—*Harry Emerson Fosdick*

It was the day before Ash Wednesday, and the teacher was telling her first graders all about receiving ashes. She carefully explained where the ashes came from, what they mean, and how the priest was going to put them on their foreheads during Mass the next day. When she was finished, she asked if they had any questions. One little girl raised her hand and asked excitedly, "Are they free?"

The little girl's question certainly shows she was a product of her society, for already, at age six, she was excited at the prospect of getting something free. But her question led me to reflect on two deeper realities of our faith. First, how lucky we are to be believers, to have the faith. For, as the *Catechism of the Catholic Church* reminds us, "Faith is a gift of God." This means our faith is not something we worked for, not something we earned. It is a gift. It is free. We might ask ourselves, how often do we thank God for the gift of faith?

Secondly, the girl's question led me to remember that no gift is ever completely free. Every gift brings with it certain responsibilities. Even the gifts freely given must be cherished and cared for. If someone gives me a plant and I don't water it, it will die. If someone gives me a delicate sweater and I throw it in the wash with my jeans, it will be ruined. Our faith, which is a free gift, must be cherished and cared for. How do we do this? By nourishing our faith with prayer, by exercising our faith through religious ritual, by practicing our faith through acts of generosity, and even, maybe, by reading a book like this.

What are some of the ways I cherish and care for my faith?

✧ God, help me to cherish and care for your free gift of faith.

30. Nearer to Thee, My God

> *Child: Grandpa, what year were you born?*
> *Grandpa: 1937.*
> *Child: Wow! If you were a baseball card,*
> *you'd be worth lots of money!*
> —Rotarian *magazine*

Tuesdays with Morrie is a beautiful book by Mitch Albom. It chronicles the meetings Albom had with a college professor of his, Morrie Schwartz. When Albom connects with his former teacher after many years, he learns that Schwartz is dying from ALS (Lou Gehrig's disease). The two men make an agreement to meet together on Tuesdays to discuss the meaning of life. With clarity, depth, humor, and sensitivity Albom narrates those visits and conversations.

The two men discuss a variety of topics: family, death, money, marriage, emotions, love, forgiveness, and so forth. On their seventh Tuesday together, they decide to talk about aging—or rather, the fear of aging. Albom begins by telling Morrie he saw dozens of billboards on his way from the airport: a cowboy smoking, a beautiful woman smiling over a shampoo bottle, a sultry teenager with her jeans unsnapped, a sexy woman in a black velvet dress. Says Albom, "Not once did I see anyone who would pass for over thirty-five."

Morrie replies, "All this emphasis on youth—I don't buy it.... Don't tell me it's so great." And he lists some of the problems his students shared with him over the years: their struggles, their feelings of inadequacy, their strife, their sense that life was miserable. But in addition to their miseries, Morrie says, the young are not wise. He puts it this way: "As you grow, you learn more. If you stayed at twenty-two, you'd always be as ignorant as you were at twenty-two." Morrie says aging is not just decay, it is growth. "It's more than the negative that you're going to die, it's also the positive that you understand you're going to die, and that you live a better life because of it."

It's tough not to envy youth. Every time I see little kids playing softball, or teenagers dancing hard and long, or younger adults reading the phone book without glasses, I think to myself, "I used to be able to do that." In aging, there are losses, yes. And we must face them. But there are gains, too. One gain is wisdom. Others, hopefully, are compassion, understanding, patience, faith. Whenever I am tempted to wish I were young again, I sing to myself the refrain of that old religious hymn: "Nearer to Thee, my God...nearer to Thee." Aging is our way of inching ever more closely toward God.

What is my attitude toward aging? Do I see it merely as decay or also as growth?

✧ God, give me a healthy attitude toward aging. Help me to see not only the losses but also the gains.

31. Butterflies Taste with Their Feet

One learns through suffering and beauty. One alone won't do.
—Anne Morrow Lindbergh

In her book, *Pilgrim at Tinker Creek,* Annie Dillard glances out her study window one day and catches sight of a host of migrating monarch butterflies. "Monarchs were everywhere," she writes. "They skittered and bobbed, rested in the air, lolled on the dust." She begins to count them, but they are more than she can number. She hurries outside to get a closer look, reporting, "Each monarch butterfly had a brittle black body and deep orange wings lined and looped in black bands." The monarchs fascinate Dillard, and conjure up for her some facts she already knows. For example, they migrate from as far north as Canada all the way to Central America—or even beyond. Monarchs are "tough and powerful, as butterflies go." Some even fly over Lake Superior without resting. Because their caterpillar stage feeds on milkweed, monarchs are foul-tasting to birds. This fact saves them from becoming an avian lunch.

At one point, Dillard coaxes one exhausted butterfly onto her index finger and lifts it to her face. She writes, "I knew those feet were actually tasting me, sipping with sensitive organs the vapors of my finger's skin; butterflies taste with their feet. All the time he held me, he opened and closed his glorious wings, senselessly, as if sighing." The migration lasts a full five days. Dillard says of those days, "Time itself was a scroll unraveled, curved and still quivering on a table or altar stone."

What does gazing at butterflies have to do with our Christian faith? A lot. Robert C. Cabot said, "When beauty overwhelms us, we are close to worship." In other words, experiencing beauty can be a way of experiencing God. In his poem, "Ode on a Grecian Urn," Keats writes this famous line, "Beauty is truth, truth beauty." Isn't God just as much beauty as God is truth? And finally, Fyodor Dostoevsky said, "The world will be saved by beauty." God can redeem us through beauty—even the beauty of one monarch butterfly.

Have I ever been overwhelmed by beauty? If so, what was that experience like for me? How do I make room for beauty in my everyday life?

✧ God of beauty, may my experience of beauty today lead me ever closer to you.

32. God Loves a Cheerful Receiver

Let it be with me according to your word. —*Luke 1:38*

Christianity is good at emphasizing the importance of giving. And well it should, for giving lies at the heart of Jesus' message. On numerous occasions he instructed his disciples to give. When sending the twelve out to preach, for example, he reminds them, "Without cost you have received; without cost you are to give" (Matthew 10:8). To the rich man who asks what he must do to follow him, Jesus says, "Go sell what you have, and give to the poor" (Mark 10:21). And St. Paul, in writing to the Corinthians, says to them, "God loves a cheerful giver" (2 Corinthians 9:7).

There is no doubt that selfless giving is integral to our faith. But, at the same time, so is selfless receiving. Selfless receiving? Isn't that a contradiction in terms? Not really. For it takes selflessness to be a gracious receiver. Why? Because in receiving, we are admitting our need. We are acknowledging our dependence. We are making ourselves vulnerable. In his book, *Living Without Gloves*, Halford Luccock gives another reason why receiving is so important. He writes, "To receive gratefully from others is to enhance others' sense of their worth."

There is yet one more reason we must learn to receive: if we do not learn to receive from others, how will we ever learn to receive from God? Receive what? Life, grace, wisdom, strength, hope, love, and consolation, to name a few things.

But receiving does not come naturally to many of us. We have to learn how to receive—that is, learn how to let things be done to and for us. This is no easy task in a society that stresses freedom, control, independence, and planning. Perhaps our model can be Mary herself, a woman who certainly knew how to give; but a woman who also knew how to say to God, "Let it be with me according to your word."

Am I a cheerful receiver? If not, what prevents me from receiving? If so, from whom have I received lately?

✧ God, please help me to be a cheerful receiver.

33. Woodward Avenue

Prayer oneth the soul to God. —Julian of Norwich

For a few years, I lived in an apartment on Woodward Avenue in Royal Oak, Michigan. Anyone familiar with Detroit knows that Woodward is the main highway linking downtown Detroit to Pontiac. For most of the way, Woodward is eight lanes wide. Where I lived the speed limit was forty-five miles per hour. When I first moved to Woodward, the noise of the traffic really bothered me. Any time of night or day, it seemed, I could hear cars, trucks, motorcycles, and buses whizzing outside my windows. People told me, "You'll get used to it." I did—but never completely.

I would sit in my living room chair each morning to pray. As I did, I would be conscious of the traffic racing by. Sometimes I would find myself saying to the traffic, "Where are you all going—and why such speed?!" That question became something of a personal mantra for me, as I directed it toward myself: "Melannie, where are you going—and why such speed?!"

The first part, "Where are you going?" became an introduction to my prayer. By asking that question, I was really asking myself, "What are your plans today? What are your hopes, your fears, your dreads, your dreams?" And I would share those with God. Then I would ask that same question only on a deeper level: "Where are you going—with your prayer, your ministry, your relationships, your life?"

The second part, "And why such speed?" was a reminder to myself to slow down. I would ask myself questions like these: "Why the rush? Must you always be trying to do more? Don't you know you can't live your whole life in one year, one month, one day, one hour?"

One day, Jesus' disciples return to him after a successful tour of preaching and healing. Jesus listens to the enthusiastic accounts of their success. Then he says those beautiful words to them, "Come aside and rest awhile" (Mark 6:31). That's exactly what prayer is, isn't it? It is a rest, a pause that gives meaning and direction to all our scurrying. More than that, prayer is a coming aside to be with Jesus.

Where am I going? And why such speed?

✧ Jesus, give direction and meaning to my scurrying today.

34. Doors

God has a way of opening doors I don't want to go through.
—Miriam Pollard, OCSO

I like Ogden Nash's observation about dogs and doors. He said, "A door is something a dog is always on the wrong side of." But dogs aren't the only ones. Sometimes we humans are on the wrong side of the door, too. Or at least we can feel as if we are.

Take those times in our lives when a door closes on us. It is a door we had planned to stroll through—perhaps confidently, eagerly—and now this: *wham!* The door slams in our face. Maybe we didn't get the job we wanted, or we lost the one we had. Or maybe we thought a relationship was going well, and all of a sudden it abruptly ended. Or maybe our customary way of acting and being in the world has suddenly proven to be hopelessly inadequate. The door slams. And we stand there staring blankly at the impenetrable wood.

Or maybe the opposite happens: a door opens and we don't want to go through it. We had gotten accustomed to the room we've been in. We know the furniture. We like the paintings on the walls. We feel at home. But now a door swings or creaks open, and we sense we are being asked to leave the familiarity of this particular place, and step over the threshold into the unknown. Maybe we are being asked to do a new kind of work, a kind for which we feel unprepared and ill-suited. Or maybe a new person enters our life extending a hand in friendship, and we hesitate to enter into this new relationship when the wounds from an old one are still red and raw. Or maybe the door is opening to the land of old age or physical diminishment and we find ourselves cowering and alone.

When we feel as if we are on the wrong side of a door, we can remember this: God is the divine doorkeeper of our lives. This means no door closes and no door opens without God's knowledge. If the opening and the closing of a particular door fills us with fear or perplexity or disbelief, let God know. Then turn to God for help and direction. And whether God bids us stay on this side of the door or go through it, know this: we do not stay or go alone.

Have I ever had a door slam in my face or open to a place I did not want to go? Did I find God on both sides of that door?

✧ God, you are the divine doorkeeper of my life.

35. Being Jesus for Others

Love ought to show itself in deeds more than in words.
—Ignatius of Loyola

As a writer, I find it hard to believe that Jesus didn't write. After all,
look at all the marvelous stories he had inside of him. "The Prodigal
Son" and "The Good Samaritan" give us only a glimpse of his great
narrative skill. His images of yeast, the mustard seed, the grain of
wheat (to name but a few) are powerful and unforgettable. When I
think of the parables and images of Jesus that are probably lost to us,
I am deeply saddened. Too bad Jesus didn't write everything down,
I say. (But sometimes I think, "Maybe that's what we other writers are
for. Maybe through our little scribblings we are somehow helping to
finish *The Complete Works of Jesus Christ."* It's a thought.)

Some people also lament the fact that Jesus was not more clear on
exactly what discipleship means. The few things he did say—like
"Deny yourself…take up your cross…follow me"—are just too nebu-
lous for some. They cry, "Can't you be more specific? Deny myself
what?…which cross?…follow you where and how?" Individuals like
these wish Jesus would have left us a few manuals like *How to be a
Disciple in Three Easy Steps* or *Church Management for Dummies.*
But to my knowledge, Jesus never wrote such books.

I, for one, am happy that Jesus and the apostles were not more
specific. After all, they lived in a world far different from our own. If
they had been more specific, we probably would be tempted to
duplicate exactly what they did and how they did it, down to wearing the same kind of sandals they wore! And if we did that, we would
end up becoming disciples for *their* people, *their* culture, and *their*
age—and what good would that do? For if our discipleship is to be
effective at all, it must speak to *our* people, *our* culture, and *our* age.
In other words, we must be disciples of Jesus in the specific circumstances in which we find ourselves. Maybe that is why, when it
comes to specifics, the gospels and epistles are deliberately vague.

But they are not vague on the essentials. Over and over again we are told—and shown—what the essence of Christian discipleship is: being Christ for others. St. Teresa of Avila summarized it so well when she wrote: "Christ has no body now on earth but yours. Yours are the eyes through which Christ looks upon the world. Yours are the feet with which he is to go about doing good. Yours are the hands with which he is to bless us now."

How am I trying to be Jesus in the specific circumstances of my life?

✧ Jesus, work through my body today—through my hands, feet, eyes, and heart!

36. Proverbs

Proverbs are short sentences drawn from long and wise experience.
—Miguel de Cervantes

I have always loved proverbs, those pithy sayings that encapsulate the wit and wisdom of a people. The Book of Proverbs in the Bible contains some memorable ones. For example, this classic: "The fear of the Lord is the beginning of wisdom" (Proverbs 9:10). There are others that my students used to like: "Like a gold ring in a pig's snout is a beautiful woman without good sense" (Proverbs 11:22). Or "Like vinegar to the teeth, and smoke to the eyes, so are the lazy to their employers" (Proverbs 10:26).

Over the years I have collected hundreds of proverbs from various lands. I offer these few for your reflection today:

- In the midst of great joy, do not promise anyone anything. In the midst of great anger, do not answer anyone's letter. (Chinese)
- The reverse side also has a reverse side. (Japanese)
- For the benefit of the flowers, we water the thorns. (Egyptian)
- Grain by grain, a loaf; stone by stone, a castle. (Bulgarian)
- To succeed, consult three old people. (Chinese)
- Speak little, speak the truth; spend little, pay cash. (German)
- If you can't do as you wish, do as you can. (Spanish)

- A lie travels around the world while the truth is putting on her shoes. (French)
- The last seven hairs are combed with special care. (Russian)
- If you wish to know what a person is, place him in authority. (Czech)
- If you run after two rabbits, you won't catch either. (Armenian)
- When a thief kisses you, count your teeth. (Yiddish)

Do any of the proverbs speak to me? In what way? What are some of my favorite proverbs?

✧ Jesus, help me to gain wisdom from those who have gone before me.

37. Getting Off a Dead Horse

God is always beyond God, the iconoclast par excellence, who over and over breaks out of the forms and symbols of our making. —Bernard Lee, SM

In a recent talk, Father Richard Fragomeni, a professor of liturgy at the Catholic Theological Union in Chicago, used an analogy that made his audience laugh. His basic advice was this: "If the horse you are riding dies, get off." He then listed a number of alternatives we try instead of facing the fact that our horse is dead and getting off. For example, we buy a stronger whip, we switch riders, we appoint a committee to study dead horses, we visit other places where they seem to be riding dead horses more effectively, or we complain about the status of dead horses these days.

Although these alternatives are amusing, they may strike a chord in those of us who have ever ridden a dead horse. Maybe, for example, we have longed to return to the past, to the so-called "good old days" when, we believe, things were so much simpler than they are now. Perhaps we have pined for the "good old" church prior to Vatican II when Mass was in Latin, priests had all the answers, and nuns dressed like "real nuns."

Sometimes the dead horse we are riding is a pet project, an idea, or a skill of ours that has seen its day. In my community, for example, we used to wear a cape with fifteen buttons running down the front. All fifteen buttons had to be covered with the same heavy black material of which the cape was made. One elderly sister performed this job. Every day she sat at her button-making machine, punching out buttons for hundreds of capes. When we started making changes in the habit, one of the first things to go were those buttons. I remember the anguish this sister went through, partly because we were changing the habit at all, but also because we were taking her job away, a job she had performed faithfully for years.

But there are dead horses far more difficult to relinquish than a button machine. One dead horse might be our image of God. Perhaps it is an image that has been shaken by current circumstances, or one that no longer challenges us to grow. Our tendency might be to keep riding that image of God even though it is dead, because the thought of getting off is too terrifying. At times like these, it is good to remember that the one who may be destroying our image of God is God. As Bernard Lee, SM, writes: "God is…the iconoclast par excellence, who over and over breaks out of the forms and symbols of our making."

Am I riding any dead horses right now? What prevents me from getting off?

✧ Loving God, be God in my life. Break out of the forms and symbols of my making.

38. If I Were the Evil Spirit

The safest road to hell is the gradual one—the gentle slope, soft underfoot, without sudden turnings, without milestones, without signposts. —C.S. Lewis

If I were the Evil Spirit, I would work very hard to prevent good people from doing good things. What tactics would I use? I would make evil attractive. I would make it easy. I would make it look natural and fun. I would convince good people that a lot of other good people were doing evil, so why not them?

If I were the Evil Spirit, I would be persistent. I would never give up and say, "I've had enough" and leave good people alone—because, who knows, the very next attempt to sway them my way might be the one that works. I would use discouragement a lot. If I couldn't get good people to actually engage in evil acts—like murder, adultery, racism—then I would discourage them from performing any good acts. How? By whispering in their ear things like this: "You're only one person, you know…what good will that do?…it's been tried before…it won't work…why waste your time?…who cares?"

If I were the Evil Spirit, I would also distract good people from doing good things. I would draw their attention to petty things. I would fool them into thinking that non-essentials were essential. I would get them to be more concerned about image than substance, process than product, institutions than people.

If I were the Evil Spirit, I would put in long hours convincing good people to fear and mistrust everything and everyone, especially God. And especially themselves. I would also try to separate good people from other good people. I would split them into factions. I have many methods at my disposal for doing this—like jealousy and pride, for example. But mostly I would rely on personal insecurity and low self-esteem. These have proven very effective throughout human history.

If I were the Evil Spirit, I would convince good people that God was far away or, if that proved impossible, then at least that God was not interested in them. I would say to them, "Do you really think the almighty God cares one iota about your puny little life?" In addition, I would convince good people that they are alone in the world. I would whisper in their ears, "No one could possibly understand what you're thinking and feeling!"

If I were the Evil Spirit I would have my work cut out for me. My job would be difficult, yes, but far from impossible.

Have any of these tactics of the Evil Spirit worked on me? Are there any other tactics I would add to these?

✧ God, deliver us from the Evil Spirit.

39. The Angelus Bell

Would you be any different if Jesus Christ did not exist?
—Anthony de Mello, SJ

I was walking in the neighborhood the other day when I heard the noon Angelus bell ring. The sound was not new to me since the church is near where I live. Though familiar, the beauty of those bells was not wasted on me. I found myself taking pleasure in listening to those clear tones with their predictable rhythm. *Bong! Bong! Bong!* (Pause.) *Bong! Bong! Bong!* (Pause.) *Bong! Bong! Bong!* (Pause.) Then, the best part of all: a whole bunch of overlapping *Bong! Bong! Bong!Bong!B!ong!Bong!B!on!g!Bong!* I found myself praying the words of the Angelus: "The angel of the Lord declared unto Mary.... Be it done unto me... And the word was made flesh." I thought: the whole purpose for ringing those bells is to remind us of the Incarnation, that single moment in time when almighty God became a human being in the womb of Mary.

Years ago, my sister bought a copy of that famous painting, "The Angelus," by Jean François Millet. It shows two peasants, a man and a woman, standing out in a wheatfield. In the distance is a church where the Angelus bell is ringing. The two peasants pause momentarily from their labor to pray. With folded hands and bowed heads, they stand reciting the Angelus together.

The Angelus is a beautiful tradition. Throughout our long history, Christians were encouraged to remember the Incarnation three times a day (six o'clock in the morning, at noon, and six o'clock in the evening). Things are different now, of course. Few of us ever hear the Angelus bell anymore. If local ordinances haven't banned its ringing altogether, then the noise of planes, traffic, refrigerators, machinery, and stereos have all but drowned it out. Although most of us no longer pray the Angelus three times a day, perhaps we can find time to pray it at least once a day.

For the fact is, the Incarnation remains the pivotal event of human history. Rosemary Haughton, in her book, *The Catholic Thing*, says that the Incarnation is a stumbling block to many. "They can accept the idea of divine immanence, God present is some sense in all things, but not the scandalous particularity of the Incarnation." The

Angelus reminds us that all history, even our own personal history, is now divinely significant.

How does my belief in the Incarnation affect the way I live my life?

✧ Jesus, give me a greater appreciation of your Incarnation and its effect on my personal history.

40. They're Just Like Me

Our love should stretch as widely across all space, and should be as equally distributed in every portion of it, as is the very light of the sun. —Simone Weil

Dan was a Jesuit novice. He was young (twenty-five), tall, handsome, and with a ready smile. He came to the Jesuits right out of a high school classroom where he was a competent and creative teacher, well-liked by his students. But when he came to the novitiate, he was asked to volunteer in a drug rehabilitation center on Detroit's east side.

In his first few days there, he was blown away. He told me, "I have absolutely nothing in common with these people." He went on to explain why. He was white, from a stable family, raised in a middle-class neighborhood, highly educated. What could he possibly say to a thirty-five-year-old high school dropout who had been using crack for fifteen years? Dan was frustrated. He felt useless. "Chatting with high schoolers about their problems at home is a far cry from counseling urban drug addicts," he said.

Two months later, Dan told a very different story. He said to me one day, "You know, all those people there—they're just like me. Deep down they have the same struggles I have, the same hopes and dreams. They want to be with their families, they love their kids, they want a decent job, they want to be responsible and free—just like me. The only difference is the drugs that are messing up their lives."

The etymology of the word "respect" is an intriguing one. It comes from the Latin *spectare* meaning "to look" and *re* which means "again." The real meaning of the word, then, is "to look again." And again. If we look hard enough, we just might see similarities and connections. Isn't this precisely what Jesus urges us to do? Isn't this what he himself did? He looked at a stooped woman and saw a dignified daughter of Abraham. He looked at a Roman centurion and saw a man of extraordinary compassion. He looked at a shady lady drawing water at a well and saw a woman thirsting for love and truth. All ministry begins with looking again. All love starts with seeing connections.

Have I ever had an experience like Dan's, where I found something in common with someone very different from myself?

✧ Jesus, help me to see how others are just like me.

41. The Kitten on the Calendar

Then you shall be radiant at what you see. —Isaiah 60:5

On my office calendar for this month there is the face of a kitten. An ordinary kitten, your garden-variety kind: butterscotch-colored fur, blue eyes, pink nose, little chin resting on white paws. All day long as I pound away on these keys, the kitten (he or she) stares down at me inquisitively.

Why do I find myself drawn to that little furry face? Cuteness is something of a magnet, I suppose. It makes me consider that if this were the only kitten God had ever made, I would give God a standing ovation and cheer, "Well done, God! Bravo! Encore!" The truth is, of course, God has the habit of giving encores even without our asking. Today it is this kitten. Tomorrow another one. And a hundred years from now, God will still be churning out kittens (if we humans don't mess things up, that is; if we don't turn our earth into a place inhospitable to kittens).

I have this same sense of gratitude when I behold other cute and beautiful things God creates: a baby's fingernail, a single daffodil, a snooping beagle, a flash of red cardinal against the snow, or one yellowish-orangish-pinkish-purplish sunset (how *does* God come up with all those colors?!). But this urge to give God a standing ovation does not rise solely from beholding things cute or beautiful. I can get equally excited over things not ordinarily seen as either: a garter snake, a praying mantis, charcoal-colored clouds, a bulb of garlic.

Emily Dickinson wrote to her cousins late in life: "'Consider the lilies' is the only commandment I ever obeyed." Some might question her level of religious fervor and argue that there are far more important commandments to obey: "Love your neighbor" and "You shall not commit adultery," for example. Maybe. Yet I think Emily was on to something, for aren't all the commandments rooted in considering things? Even the love of a neighbor or a spouse is nourished by daily considerations. "Consider the lilies," Jesus tells us (Luke 12:27). Perhaps we could expand that exhortation to include other things as well. Consider the kittens…consider the children…consider the bulbs of garlic…consider the rivers…consider the refugees…consider the dying…consider everything.

What or whom do I already consider in my life? What or whom do I need to consider more?

✧ Jesus, help me to be more considerate of everything and everyone I encounter today.

42. Making Unpopular Decisions

The truth will ouch. —*Arnold Glasow*

We all know people who have made unpopular decisions. Probably we ourselves have been there more than once: the parent who says "no" to her daughter's request. The teacher who gives the failing grade. The principal who does not renew the contract of a popular teacher. The pastor who goes against the recommendation of his parish council. The bishop who closes a parish.

Most of us don't make unpopular decisions for the fun of it. We don't wake up in the morning and say, "Let's see, what decision can I make today that will really turn everyone against me?" Or "What decision can I make today that will make me look like a total jerk?" No, most of us who give thoughtful consideration to the decisions we make tend to agonize over the unpopular ones. Along the way to making one, we might try to talk ourselves out of it by saying things like: "Just let things be...give it more time...it's no big deal...let someone else make that decision." But then there comes a time when we see clearly (or clear enough) that we have to make an unpopular decision, and we do. As a result, we might be met with jeering crowds, slamming doors, angry tears, irate phone calls, cold stares, anonymous notes. Yes, it is not easy to make unpopular decisions.

Jesus made them. Over and over again the gospels show him making unpopular decisions. For example, he picked ordinary individuals to be his disciples ("He has no sense of propriety!"). He embraced lepers ("He's foolhardy!"). He conversed with women on the streets ("Who does he think they are—people?"). He ate with tax collectors ("He's disloyal!"). He cured on the sabbath ("He has no respect for the law!"). He even headed back to Jerusalem where he knew his enemies were waiting for him ("He's crazy!"). Jesus put his reputation on the line with many of the decisions he made. He knew, as we do too, that one's reputation can be a small price to pay for doing the right thing. Jesus also knew that sometimes a life is the only fitting sacrifice to make for goodness and truth.

Have I ever had to make an unpopular decision? What was this like for me?

✧ Jesus, be with me in all my decisions today—even the unpopular ones.

43. Uncle Marty

Who owns a garden...is very close to God. —K. Edelman

Uncle Marty was a tall, barrel-chested man, the father of five. He lived life in sweeping gestures. His laugh was loud and his opinions were strong, though not immutable. In addition to his family, he had one passion: his garden. In his later years, arthritis assaulted his once strapping body. Toward the end, he was so crippled he could not walk unaided. Yet he still kept his garden.

It was Memorial Day when Uncle Marty hobbled out to the backyard to get his tomato plants in, a task he had done virtually every year of his life. He used his cane to get to the garden, but once there, he laid it aside and dropped to his knees. The pain in his back and hips was so bad, any type of bending over was impossible. So instead, he crawled around on his hands and knees and planted his tomato plants, all forty-eight of them. Relieved and proud, he put away his tools, washed up, and settled down in front of the TV to watch the start of the Indy 500 with three of his grandchildren at his feet. He was explaining to them some detail about the pace car when he had an intestinal rupture.

When his daughter Kathy got to the hospital, she found her father, though in severe pain, vehemently refusing the nurse's request to remove his wedding band for surgery. The nurse finally gave in and stuck a piece of tape over the ring. That victory was Uncle Marty's last. Seven days later, he died.

His family was stunned. As they planned the funeral, Kathy found herself wondering what kind of floral arrangement would truly honor her father. Roses? Carnations? No. Suddenly, she knew what to do. Digging up a few tomato plants from her own garden, she put them into a pot. Then she begged her neighbors, through her tears, for a few of their young corn plants. They said, "Honey, take as many as you want." She planted the corn with the tomatoes. At the wake, this unique bouquet was a perfect tribute to the man who so deeply loved his garden.

Some of us are roses and carnations people. And that's fine. But others are corn and tomatoes people. And that's good, too.

How do I acknowledge and respect the uniqueness of my loved ones?

✧ God, help me to acknowledge and respect the uniqueness of the individuals I meet today.

44. Making Others Look Good

*Everyone flocked about (Melanie), for who can resist
the charm of one who discovers in others admirable
qualities undreamed of even by themselves.*
—*Margaret Mitchell, in* Gone with the Wind

Someone once said, "Truly great dancers are those who make their partners look good." Fred Astaire was a truly great dancer. He could make any partner look good. Remember the time he danced with a wooden coat tree? There he was, waltzing with it, swaying beside it, gliding around it, twirling it with the tips of his fingers. First he nudged it away, then he coaxed it back again. You would have sworn the thing was alive. You saw the coat tree bending (or so it seemed!), then gliding under its own power (not really!). By the end of the dance, you were convinced that the wooden coat tree was one of the best dancers you had ever seen!

What a gift it is, to make others look good. Jesus had that gift. He made others look good all the time. He made Simon look good the day he said to him, "You are Peter, and upon this rock I will build my church" (Matthew 16:18). By saying these words, Jesus made a lowly fisherman look like a great religious leader. Another time, Jesus saw a poor widow dropping two tiny coins into the temple treasury. He said of her, "I tell you truly, this poor widow put in more than all the rest" (Luke 21:3). Jesus made this destitute woman look like a wealthy benefactor. And once, Jesus was entering Jericho and spotted a tax collector named Zacchaeus perched in a sycamore tree (Luke 19:2–10). Through the sharing of a single meal with the man, Jesus ended up making a greedy traitor look like a generous loyalist.

There is a vast difference, however, between what Astaire did for that coat tree and what Jesus did for people. With Astaire, the coat tree only *looked* like a graceful dancer. It remained a coat tree. With Jesus, the individuals did not merely look better than they were. They actually *became* better than they were before. Peter became a great leader, the widow became a generous donor, Zacchaeus became an honest man. Jesus had the power not only to make others look good; he had the power to make people become better than they were.

Jesus can do that for us today. He can make us better than we are.

All we need to do is to let go of whatever it is that holds us back. Peter had to let go of his fishing boat and nets. The widow had to let go of those two coins, that is, all she had to live on. Zacchaeus first had to let go of the security of that sycamore tree. Then he had to let go of his former way of life.

What holds me back from being a better person? How can I make others look good and become better?

✦ Jesus, help me to become a better person today.

45. How Dangerous Am I?

Life is either a daring adventure or it is nothing. —Helen Keller

J. Edgar Hoover once called Martin Luther King, Jr., "the most dangerous man in America." Hoover was right, although perhaps not in the way he supposed. King was a dangerous man. All prophets are. Why? Because they speak out against the *status quo;* they cry out for a change in the way things are. Prophets advocate revolution. And advocating revolution, even through peaceful means, is always dangerous.

Jesus was a dangerous man. In the fourth chapter of the Gospel of Mark, right after Jesus cures the man with the withered hand, we read: "The Pharisees went out and immediately took counsel with the Herodians against him to put him to death" (Mark 3:6). This is only the third chapter, mind you! Jesus has barely begun his ministry and already his enemies are plotting not merely to shush him up, but to silence him—forever! We can almost hear the leader of the Pharisees saying to the Herodians solemnly, "He is the most dangerous man in Galilee."

What about us who claim to be followers of Jesus? Are we supposed to be dangerous too? The answer is "yes." For if we are truly living our faith, we can never be fully satisfied with the way things are. We can never be satisfied with ourselves, for example. We can never say, "I'm very content with how I'm living my faith," or "I think I'm as good as I need to get." We must continually appraise the way we are living our faith.

We can never be completely satisfied with our church, either. Instead, we must dare to criticize the way we Christians are collectively living our faith. Halford Luccock, writing in the *Christian Herald*, shows us how to do this when he writes, "Christianity has grown soft, sentimental, saccharine; it has become too much flute and too little trumpet."

In her book, *Walking on Water*, Madeleine L'Engle says we must question our traditional religious beliefs continually, "otherwise, like those of the church establishment of Galileo's day, we truly become God's frozen people." One of the greatest threats to living out our Christian faith is complacency. One of the greatest goals is to become as dangerous as Jesus.

How satisfied am I with the way I am personally living out my faith? How satisfied am I with the church?

✧ Jesus, help me to become as dangerous as you.

46. Stay Awake

What was your word, Jesus?
Love? Affection? Forgiveness?
All your words were
One word: Wakeup.
—Antonio Machado

The theme of sleeping and waking permeates Scripture. Did you even notice how many times God (or an angel) comes to individuals while they are asleep? Jacob encountered an angel of the Lord in the middle of the night and wrestled with the celestial being until dawn (Genesis 32:23–33). The young Samuel was asleep in the temple when the Lord woke him not once, but three times (1 Samuel 3:1–18). The prophet Elijah, fleeing for his life from the wicked Queen Jezebel, fell asleep under a broom tree when an angel of the Lord shook him awake and served him breakfast (1 Kings 19:5–8). Joseph too encountered an angel as he slept restlessly one night, trying to decide what to do about Mary (Matthew 1:20).

The symbolism in these stories is profound. In each instance, God is not merely waking these individuals up *from* something, from their natural sleep. God is waking them up *to* something: to a deeper intimacy with God and to a new direction for their lives. Jacob has his name changed to Israel by the angel. Samuel is commissioned to be God's prophet. Elijah, who had begged for death, is instructed to eat and to continue his journey of life. And Joseph is told the true origin of Mary's child and is directed to take her as his wife.

The night before he dies, Jesus takes Peter, James, and John with him to the garden of Gethsemane. He says to them, "Stop here and stay awake" (Mark 14:34), while he goes further into the garden to pray. We all know what happens next. While Jesus undergoes his agony in the garden, the apostles fall asleep. When Jesus returns and finds them sleeping, he asks, "Were you not able to stay awake one hour?" Then he says to them, "Stay awake, all of you; and pray" (Mark 14:37–38).

In his book, *Fathoming Bethlehem*, Bishop Robert Morneau writes that all of Jesus' ministry was essentially "a wakeup call." In fact, continues Morneau, spirituality itself is easy to define: "Just stay awake!"

Have I ever felt wakened to a deeper intimacy with God and/or to a new direction for my life?

✧ Jesus, let me hear your wakeup call for me this day.

47. Who Is God?

> *It is both terrible and comforting to dwell in the inconceivable nearness of God. —Karl Rahner, SJ*

One way to get to know someone better is to learn what others say about that person. The observations of others can deepen our understanding and appreciation of someone else—even someone we may already know quite well. The same principle operates in our quest to know God better. We have a certain understanding of who God is based on our own experience, true. But why not enrich and expand that understanding by listening to others? This meditation simply gathers together some observations individuals have made about God.

- God is the minimum as well as the maximum. (Nicholas of Cusa)

- For once you have begun to walk with God, you need only keep on walking with God, and all of life becomes one long stroll—such a marvelous feeling. (Etty Hillesum)

- God is the all-sufficient explanation, the eternal rapture glimpsed in every Archimedean cry of "Eureka!" (Bernard Lonergan)

- When I went to Uganda, I thought I was taking my male, white, cool, dry British God to those people. But I found God already there among the Masai people—a warm, moist, and salty God. (Edwina Gateley)

- God is really only another artist. (Pablo Picasso)

- Now, God's not a fast person, he is a sure person. Swiftness is not God's best thing. (A woman in Harlem)

- There is nothing better as an antidote to narcissism than meeting the living God. (William Barry, SJ)

- Who wants to swim far in the spiritual ocean if God turns out to be a shark? (John P. Gorsuch)

- I fled from God and God came with me. (St. Anselm of Canterbury)

- God is sheer, exuberant, relational aliveness…inexhaustible source of new being…ground of hope for the whole created universe. (Elizabeth Johnson)

Do any of these quotes resonate with my own experience of God?

✧ God, help me to know you better today.

48. Thorns Have Roses

Some people are always grumbling because roses have thorns;
I am thankful that thorns have roses. —Alphonse Karr

Helen, an eighty-three-year-old widow, invited two of her widow friends over for Sunday dinner and a football game. After dinner, she insisted that her two friends watch the football game while she cleared up in the kitchen. A few minutes later she heard her friends cheering and screaming. Curious, Helen ran into the living room to see what the excitement was all about—forgetting that she had left the water running in the sink. Twenty minutes later when she returned to the kitchen, she was horrified to find several inches of water all over the floor. Immediately the three women began to mop up the water, but it had already leaked down into the apartment below.

A few minutes later the doorbell rang. It was Jean, the young woman who lived below. She introduced herself to Helen and offered to help clean up the mess. Afterward, Helen got to talking with Jean and learned that she had two small children (ages two and six months) and that her husband had been unemployed for six months. The next day, Helen flew into action. She called her local parish and told them about this needy family. Soon, food donations arrived for them. In addition, a few temporary job offers came for Jean's husband. Commenting on the incident later, Helen said, "God let me forget to turn off that water so I could meet Jean and learn of her need."

The old proverb says, "Every cloud has a silver lining." Another way of looking at it is this: God can use anything to bring about good—even our forgetfulness.

Have I ever experienced a silver lining in a cloud or a rose among the thorns? If so, what was that experience like for me?

✧ God, help me to see more clearly how you can use anything to bring about good!

49. Kissing the Earth with Our Feet

Walk as if you are kissing the earth with your feet.
—Thich Nhat Hahn

Years ago I helped work the switchboard at the main entrance of our provincial house. One day a gentleman came to see a sister. Since she was going to be tied up for a few minutes, the man sat down in the hall to wait. As he did, he watched the sisters passing back and forth, back and forth. Some were on their way to chapel, others were going to offices, and still others were going outside or coming back in again. After several minutes, the man came back to me and said, "Can I ask you something?" "Sure," I said. He asked, "How come everyone's running?"

His question surprised me, for I hadn't noticed anyone running. As far as I was concerned, the nuns were walking the way they always walked, as I always walked. But after the man left, I started to pay more attention to the sisters as they went by the switchboard, and sure enough! I had to admit it: most of them were running—or, at least, they were going pretty fast.

That was years ago. I think many of us have learned to slow down since then. But still, when I give talks or retreats I often ask people if they tend to walk fast—especially when they are at work or when they are running errands. (Notice, we do not say walking errands!) Most people admit they do. Half teasingly, I say, "Did you know that you can tell how important people are by how fast they walk? The faster they walk, the more important they are!" Of course, we really do not believe that, but, sometimes we act as if we do. It is almost as if we are announcing our importance by the speed with which we move. (If we are really honest, we also know that by walking fast we discourage people from stopping us and giving us more work to do!)

It is not simply that we walk so fast either: it is that we walk so hard. *Stomp, stomp, stomp!* My reflecting on this led me to conclude that our Christian faith—with its emphasis on the sacredness of both time and place—calls us to walk slowly and gently on this earth. The Buddhist monk Thich Nhat Hahn said something similar. He observed that when we walk fast and hard, "we print anxiety and sorrow on the earth." He suggests we all walk more slowly and gently. "Walk as if you are kissing the earth with your feet," he says.

How do I walk on this earth: slowly and gently or "stomp, stomp, stomp"? How do I feel about the way I walk?

✦ God, help me to walk as if I am kissing the earth with my feet.

50. Religion: Theory or Love Affair?

*"I think, therefore I am," is the statement of an intellectual
who underrates toothaches. —Milan Kundera*

For some people, faith is an intellectual endeavor consisting primarily of the pursuit of truth. For such individuals, faith is essentially creedal. It is believing in God, the Trinity, the Immaculate Conception, the Incarnation, the resurrection, heaven and hell, the communion of saints, the forgiveness of sins, and life everlasting, amen.

Though our faith certainly includes an intellectual component (look at our fine tradition of education), it cannot remain a cerebral assent that ignores the rest of our person or the day-to-day world in which we live. No, our faith, if it is genuine, permeates our entire being. It enlightens our minds, enlivens our hearts, and directs our hands and feet in specific acts of love.

No parable illustrates this point more clearly than the parable of the Good Samaritan (Luke 10:29–37). Jesus said that a certain Jew was on the road to Jericho when he was attacked by hoodlums. They beat him up, robbed him, and left him half-dead in the ditch. Both a priest and a Levite came along and, seeing the man lying there, passed him by. Then a Samaritan happened by. He, too, was on his way to somewhere. He wasn't out for the fun of it; he had work to do, plans. His "to do" list that day did not include: "Pick up half-dead man from ditch."

Yet when he spots the man, he stops. He makes room on his agenda for this unexpected and terribly inconvenient situation. Why? Because he "was moved with compassion at the sight." In other words, he did not have to consult some creed to find out what was expected of him in this particular situation. He did not have to look up "half-dead Jews" in some law book to find out what to do. No, his own heart told him what to do. The Samaritan's love was not theoretical; it was spontaneous, active, personal, and real.

G.K. Chesterton said it well: "Let your religion be less of a theory and more of a love affair."

Is my religion more theory or more love affair? How can I tell?

✧ Jesus, help my love to be more spontaneous, active, personal, and real.

60

51. Difficult People

The Bible tells us to love our neighbors, and also to love our enemies, probably because they are generally the same people.
—G.K. Chesterton

We have all experienced "difficult" people, that is, those individuals who annoy us, upset us, or get in our way. We meet them everywhere—in our families, in our religious communities, at work, in our parishes, and in our neighborhoods. Jesus commanded us to love everyone, which of course includes even difficult people. But did he give us any practical advice on how we might deal with them? Yes, he did, mostly through his own example.

Jesus knew his fair share of difficult people. First there were his fellow Nazareans, the neighbors he had known since childhood. Shortly after Jesus begins his public ministry, he returns to Nazareth for a visit (Luke 4:16–30). During a sabbath service he reprimands the townspeople for their lack of faith in him. So outraged are they by what he says, they try to push him off a cliff! What does Jesus do? Does he take back what he said? Does he try to reason with the people? No. He simply walks away from them. From that moment on Jesus sets up his base of operations not in Nazareth, but in Capernaum. The lesson is clear: sometimes the best way to deal with difficult people—even those close to us—is to walk away from them, especially if they are preventing us from carrying out our mission in life.

Another time a certain Samaritan village refuses to offer hospitality to Jesus and his disciples (Luke 9:51–56). His disciples are indignant and say to him, "Lord, do you want us to call down fire from heaven to consume them?" Jesus rebukes them for their vengeful attitude and tells them they will simply go to another village to preach. His message is this: we must resist the temptation to "zap" difficult people. If we are secure in what we are about, we do not have to wage war every time somebody crosses or insults us.

On a number of occasions Jesus openly confronts difficult people—most notably, the scribes and Pharisees. He listens to their questions and asks his own. He challenges them and speaks out against their legalism and hypocrisy. By doing so, Jesus reminds us that sometimes we are called to dialogue with difficult people too. How do we know when to walk away from such individuals and when to dialogue with them? There is no simple answer, of course. Each situation requires discernment rooted in prayer such as this: "Jesus, give me the strength to walk away from difficult people and the courage to stay and dialogue with them. And give me the wisdom to know which to do. Amen."

How am I dealing with the difficult people in my life?

✧ Jesus, help me to love everyone you put into my life—even the difficult people.

52. The One-Inch Picture Frame

Writing a novel is like driving a car at night. You can see only as far as your headlights, but you can make the whole trip that way.
—E.L. Doctorow

In her book, *Bird by Bird*, Anne Lamott talks about writing. She describes how sometimes, when she sits down to write, she begins to panic at the prospect of writing another book. That's when she notices the one-inch picture frame on her desk. She tells how she put that frame there to remind herself "that all I have to do is to write down as much as I can see through a one-inch picture frame." In other words, instead of trying to write the entire book, Lamott tries to write only one paragraph instead.

Lamott's picture frame is a good symbol for how we should live our lives, too: one square inch at a time, that is, one day at a time. That phrase "one day at a time" is not completely accurate, however, for we really live our lives only one moment at a time—this moment. We sometimes forget that and try to live our entire life all at once. We wake up in the morning, for example, and before we have even finished brushing our teeth we are fretting over something that happened two days ago or something that might happen tomorrow. Or we plan a vacation and before we have even decided where we are going, we are worrying about our luggage getting lost or our travelers' checks being stolen. We are changing the baby's diaper, and we find ourselves troubled over how we are ever going to afford to send him to college.

The book of Genesis tells us that God created the world in "six days." God certainly didn't need six days. God could have created everything in one day—or a single instant, for that matter. Perhaps the six days of creation are meant to remind us that we, who are made in the image and likeness of God, are meant to do our own work of creation in segments too, in daily allotments. In fact, one of God's greatest gifts to us may very well be the dividing of time into days. Have I thanked God for sunsets and dawns lately?

Do I ever try to live my life all at once? Am I attentive to the present moment or am I always fretting about yesterday or worrying about tomorrow?

✦ God, help me to live my life one day at a time, for I truly believe that you are with me all my days!

53. Children

Pretty much all the honest truth-telling there is in the world is done by children. —Oliver Wendell Holmes

Little Zachary burst in the door and excitedly announced to his mother that he had won a prize in his first-grade class. His mother told him how proud she was of him, and then asked what he had done to achieve the prize. "I won," he said, "for having the oldest mom in the whole class!"

Children like Zachary can be remarkably honest. They can be perceptive as well. Angela Schwindt wrote, "While we try to teach our children all about life, our children teach us what life is all about." Let us listen to a few lessons about life from the following children:

• A pajama-clad little girl said to her parents, "I'm going to say my prayers now. Anyone want anything?"

• Teacher: "If you have two dollars, and you ask your father for four dollars, how much will you have?"
Billy: "Two dollars."

Teacher: "You don't know your math."
Billy: "You don't know my father."

• Father to his first-grade son: "What does your new teacher look like?"
Child: "Just like my kindergarten teacher, only with a different head."

• As the little boy and his mother were riding down the escalator, the boy asked, "Mom, what happens when the basement gets full of steps?"

• The six-year-old girl was thrilled to attend her first wedding. She watched as the pastor, groom, and three groomsmen took their places up front. Then she turned around and watched wide-eyed as the bride came up the aisle. Suddenly, she turned to her father and whispered, "Daddy, does she get to take her pick?"

• The Sunday school teacher was taking the story of the Prodigal Son with her third graders. After telling them the story, she asked, "And who was not happy that the prodigal son returned home?" One little girl replied, "The fatted calf."

What lessons about life have I learned from children lately?

✧ Jesus, you said, "Let the little children come to me." Help me to welcome children into my life too.

54. Serenity

> *Serenity comes not alone by removing the outward causes and occasions of fear, but by the discovery of inward reservoirs to draw upon. —Rufus Jones*

Whenever we experience distress, our immediate response is to turn to someone outside of ourselves for help. We probably did this instinctively as a child. When we fell and scraped our knee, for instance, we ran to our mother with the hope that she would make it "all better." As a teenager, if we suffered a heartache, we probably turned to a close friend or an older sibling for help and comfort.

As Christian adults, many of us are in the habit of turning immediately to God when troubles beset us. And this is good. It is good for us to ask God to remove those things in our lives that disturb our serenity. Maybe it is our own compulsiveness, a strained relationship, an economic hardship, or illness. But sometimes when we ask God to take our troubles away, God seems to say no. At times like this, we can recall the wisdom of the quote at the beginning of this meditation. Perhaps God is leading us to discover inward reservoirs we didn't know we had. God might be saying, "You are stronger than you think."

Or God could be saying, "There is goodness in this trying situation that you do not see yet. But I see it. Trust me." In his letter to the Corinthians, St. Paul tells of experiencing a "thorn in the flesh." We do not know for sure what this thorn was. Some say it might have been a physical disability, a severe temptation, or even a strong opponent. Whatever it was, Paul begs God three times to remove this thorn, but God does not. Instead, God says to him, "My grace is sufficient for you, for power is made perfect in weakness" (2 Corinthians 12:7–9).

Have I ever experienced a "thorn in the flesh"? Have I ever experienced God saying to me, "My grace is sufficient for you"?

✧ Jesus, give me your strength to endure the "thorns" in my life today.

55. Pencil Marks on a Door Frame

There is nothing like returning to a place that remains unchanged to find the ways in which you yourself have altered.
—*Nelson Mandela*

The other day I came across a spiritual book which I had not read in twenty-five years. As soon as I saw it, I got a warm feeling inside. Twenty-five years ago, this was one of my favorite books; I remember not being able to put it down. Every sentence seemed to jump out at me. One chapter in particular I almost memorized. The book made a tremendous impact on me. It set me on fire.

I took the book and began to read it again, hoping to rekindle some of those feelings I had in my youth. But as I read it slowly and prayerfully, something happened. More to the point, *nothing* happened. Oh sure, it was still a decent book, well written and solid. But it no longer had the power it once had over me. It no longer set me on fire. Why? Not because the book had changed, but because I had changed. I was no longer the person I was twenty-five years ago.

The old maxim says, "You cannot dip your toe into the same river twice." How true. But it's not just because the river keeps changing. So does your toe! This incident with the book could have made me feel guilty: "I'm not as holy as I used to be." Or it could have made me feel sad: "I wish I could get back those feelings I had twenty-five years ago!" Instead, the incident made me feel immensely grateful. I found myself thanking God for this book (and its author!), for the fact remains: this book *did* have a tremendous impact on my spiritual life. I also thanked God for the growth I detected in myself as I read this book again. I said to God, "I guess I have come a long way since then." Then I corrected myself: "I guess *we* have come a long way since then!"

As children, we measured our physical growth by pencil marks on a door frame. As adults, we can sometimes measure our spiritual growth by the books that set us on fire.

Have I ever experienced the truth of Mandela's words at the beginning of this meditation? What are some of the ways I measure my spiritual growth?

✧ God, you and I have come a long way together. For this, I am most grateful!

56. A Choice of Attitude

I discovered I always have choices, and sometimes it's only a choice of attitude. —Judith M. Knowlton

A businessman hired an advertising company to help him sell his product. The first question the ad man asked him was, "What do you sell?" The man replied, "Mattresses." "No you don't," said the ad man.

"You sell sweet dreams and good sex."

The anecdote illustrates a familiar adage: it all depends on how you look at it. In other words, the way we look at things—that is, our attitude—can make all the difference in the world. Jesus knew the significance of attitude. In fact, many of his teachings were nothing more (and nothing less!) than a radical change in attitude. One incident in his life that illustrates this point beautifully is the cure of the crippled woman (Luke 13:10–17).

The story begins with Jesus teaching in the synagogue on the sabbath. In his audience is a woman who has been crippled for eighteen years. We are told "she was bent over, completely incapable of standing erect." When Jesus sees her, he is moved with compassion and says to her, "Woman, you are set free of your infirmity." He lays his hands on her and at once she stands up straight and begins to glorify God. The crowd is in awe at what Jesus has done.

But the scribes and Pharisees are not in awe. They are outraged that Jesus has cured this woman on the sabbath. Angrily, the leader of the synagogue says to the woman and to the crowd, "There are six days when work should be done. Come on those days to be cured, not on the sabbath."

The story portrays conflicting attitudes: toward the woman, toward sickness, and toward the sabbath. On the one hand we have the scribes and Pharisees who view the woman as something of a nuisance. After all, she is "only" a woman, and a sick one at that. But Jesus' attitude toward her is very different. He calls her a "daughter of Abraham," that is, a fellow believer deserving of love and respect. The scribes and Pharisees see physical illness as a punishment for sin and are unmoved by this woman's condition. Jesus sees her infirmity as pitiful and is moved with compassion to bring her relief.

Jesus' attitude toward the sabbath was also notably different from that of the scribes and Pharisees. They had reduced the sabbath to the rigid observance of detailed laws. By his healing, Jesus celebrates the real purpose of the sabbath: the freeing of individuals from the bondage of Satan.

Have I ever experienced a radical change in my attitude? What attitudes might Jesus be calling me to change today?

✧ Jesus, give me your attitude toward everything.

57. The Penance of Inconvenience

No one knows his or her true character until he or she has run
out of gas, purchased something on the installment plan,
and raised an adolescent. —Lorene Workman

When we hear the word "penance" we usually think of sacrifices we freely make for God; for example, fasting for a day, going to daily Mass during Lent, contributing to the parish building fund. Sometimes the penances we do, however, are not freely chosen; they are thrust upon us by circumstances. Perhaps our penance is to work through difficulties in a relationship, to care for an ill loved one, or to endure physical pain. But more often than not, the penances that life sets before us are of a lesser degree. One such penance we face every day is inconvenience.

The etymology of the word "inconvenience" is an interesting one. It comes from two Latin words: *in*, meaning "not," and *convenire*, meaning "to come together." Thus, an inconvenience occurs when things do not come together for us, when they don't go as we would like them to go. For instance, we settle down to watch TV and the picture is fuzzy. Or we plan a weekend getaway for the family only to have our youngest come down with the measles. Or we're coasting along on a three-lane highway when we suddenly see an orange sign that says, "Left two lanes closed ahead."

Inconvenience as a form of penance can help us to grow spiritually. First, it can keep us humble. Every time we are inconvenienced, we are reminded that we are not in control of our lives. This reminder can deepen the realization of our dependency on others—and on God.

Secondly, daily inconveniences make demands on our love. In fact, most inconveniences are directly related to loving others. We endure the inconvenience of standing in the grocery checkout line, for example, because we are buying food for our family whom we love. We willingly put up with the terrible inconvenience of 2:00 a.m. feedings out of love for our new baby.

In the spiritual life, it is selfishness that causes death. And, if we are not careful, selfishness can creep into our lives step by step, convenience by convenience. By embracing the penance of inconvenience, we hinder the encroachment of selfishness while simultaneously growing in humility and love.

What are some of the inconveniences in my life that are keeping me humble and calling me to greater love?

✧ God, help me to practice well the penance of inconvenience today.

58. Two by Two

> *Elizabeth Barrett Browning: "What is the secret of your life? Tell me, that I may make my life beautiful too."*
> *Charles Kingsley: "I had a friend."*

Brielle and Kyrie Jackson, twin girls, were born twelve weeks early. As was standard hospital practice, the little girls were placed in separate incubators. Kyrie, the larger twin at two pounds three ounces, quickly began to gain weight. But little Brielle, weighing only two pounds, had breathing and heart problems. Two weeks after birth, Brielle's condition became critical.

The nurses did everything they could to stabilize Brielle. They suctioned her breathing passages and turned up the flow of oxygen into the incubator. But the baby squirmed restlessly and her heartbeat soared. It was then that one of the nurses remembered a procedure, common in parts of Europe, that called for putting newborn twins in the same crib. The nurse secured the permission of the twins' parents to try the procedure.

She placed little Brielle into the incubator with her sister. No sooner had she closed the incubator door than Brielle snuggled up to Kyrie. Immediately she calmed down. Within minutes her blood-oxygen readings were the best they had been since her birth. Within days she was gaining weight. Eventually, both babies were healthy and strong enough to go home. Today a handful of institutions in this country are adopting the practice of double-bedding.

In the gospel of Mark we read: "(Jesus) called the twelve and began to send them out two by two" (Mark 6:7). Jesus knew that we draw great strength and support from those with whom we share a common journey. We can well thank God for the gift of nurturing we receive through our relationships with both family and friends.

Who walks beside me as I journey through life? Whom do I encourage and support with my friendship?

> ✧ Jesus, I know I can't go it alone. Thank you for the friends you have given me who make my life more beautiful.

59. You Don't Have Time to Pray?

Wherever you are, whether in your room or any other place, pray. At once that spot becomes a church. —St. Bernard

You don't have time to pray. The kids are jumping up and down on the bed, your husband can't find any socks, and the car needs an oil change. Your cousin in Chicago is ill. Your mother keeps asking, "When are you coming to see me?" The dog needs to be walked, you have three bags of clothing you should take to St. Vincent de Paul, and you think you might need new glasses. Babies are starving in Africa, bombs are going off in Northern Ireland, and your son's teacher wants to see you. Your lower back hurts. You lost your rosary six months ago, the binding on your Bible just split in two, and you've got to stop eating donuts. You're a eucharistic minister for the 7:30 a.m. Mass on Sunday morning, and Kroeger's is having a special on macaroni and cheese. You're having a personality conflict with someone at work, you're out of milk, your daughter is acting a little strange, and you need a haircut. You want to go to the parish mission, the young couple across the street can't get pregnant, you're convinced life is passing you by, and you can't balance your checkbook.

You don't have time to pray? Sit down. Close your eyes. Take a deep breath. And pray. Pray what? Pray anything. Tell God you don't have time to pray. Tell God you think you're losing it. Tell God to help you. Tell Jesus you love him. Tell the Holy Spirit to give you wisdom. Tell Mary to walk with you. But pray. Pray for yourself. Pray for your family. Pray for Northern Ireland. Pray for the young couple across the street. Pray, pray, pray. Even if you can afford only three-and-a-half minutes right now. Pray.

With prayer (as with life) there is no such thing as perfection. There is no perfect time to pray, no perfect place to pray, no perfect way to pray. Be flexible. Try praying anywhere, anytime, anyhow. Try praying while brushing your teeth in the morning, while sitting in the car getting an oil change, while waiting in line at the bank, while walking to the mailbox. Try praying in places you may never have prayed before. Try the kitchen table, the shower, a park bench, a library, the dentist's waiting room. Try praying while you're doing other things like changing the baby's diaper, sipping cappuccino, walking the dog, reading the comics, stirring tapioca, pressing a shirt, washing the car, vacuuming the family room.

In his book, *To Be a Pilgrim*, Basil Hume wrote these consoling words, "Trying to pray is prayer, and it is very good prayer."

Where and how am I trying to pray?

✦ God, help me to pray today.

60. The Huggers and the Hiders

> *Grace is the fact that God never leaves us alone.*
> —*Charles Stinnette, Jr.*

Sister Kathleen is an assistant principal and guidance counselor in an elementary school in Cleveland's inner city. She works mostly with the youngest children in the school. Every day she visits the lunch room and the playground for, as she says, "I'm a strong believer in the power of 'informal presence' with the kids."

Sister Kathleen says you can almost divide the children into two groups: the huggers and the hiders. When she walks into the lunch-room, for example, immediately the huggers jump up, run to her, and throw their little arms around her. Their hands are often covered with part of their lunch. On some days it's peanut butter and jelly. On pizza days, it's tomato sauce. Sister welcomes the hugs, though, saying to herself, "Whatever is now on the back of my skirt will come off in the wash."

Then there are the hiders, those children who go out of their way to avoid her. When Sister walks out onto the playground, for example, the hiders run away from her. Their flight is often caused by a guilty conscience. Chances are the hiders are those kids who just stole someone else's ball, just said a bad word, or just gave another kid a big shove. Calmly and patiently, Sister seeks out these hiders, saying, "I want these kids to see me as someone who cares for them, not as someone they see only when they're in trouble."

When it comes to our relationship with God, aren't we huggers and hiders too? Some days we are huggers who run eagerly into God's arms. Other days, like Adam and Eve after they ate the apple, we are hiders who fearfully run away from God. Our consolation (and our salvation!) lies in the fact that God always seeks us, patiently and lovingly. As St. John of the Cross said, "If we are seeking God, our Beloved is seeking us much more."

When it comes to my relationship with God, am I a hugger or a hider or both?

✧ Seeker God, help me to seek you.

61. The Psalms: The Real Thing

What is more pleasing than a psalm? —St. Ambrose

I love the psalms. These ancient prayers possess the power to move me deeply. These lines, for example, never fail to calm my anxiety: "The Lord is my light and my salvation; whom shall I fear? The Lord is the stronghold of my life; of whom shall I be afraid?" (Psalm 27:1).

I love the psalms because they articulate the wide range of moods I experience in my own journey of life. They express my low times: "My life is spent in sorrow, and my years with sighing; my strength fails...and my bones waste away" (Psalm 31:10). They express my high times: "Your deeds, O Lord, have made me glad; for the work of your hands I shout with joy!" (Psalm 92:4–5). The psalms are extremely realistic, reminding me of my sin: "For I know my transgressions, and my sin is ever before me" (Psalm 51:3), and reminding me of God's mercy: "O purify me, then I shall be clean; O wash me, I shall be whiter than snow" (Psalm 51:7).

The psalms recall God's power and gentleness: "By your strength you established the mountains...you silence the roaring of the seas...you visit the earth and water it...softening it with showers, and blessing its growth" (Psalm 65: 6–7, 9–10). They are filled with gratitude for God's favors: "You have turned my mourning into dancing; you have taken off my sackcloth and clothed me with joy" (Psalm 30:11). In unforgettable images, the psalms hold before me my deepest desires and longings. "Like the deer that yearns for running streams, so my soul is yearning for you, my God" (Psalm 42:1).

In her book, *Undercurrents*, Martha Manning says this about the psalms: "It's incredible to me that we never learned the psalms as children. All that time and energy memorizing the catechism when the real thing was right here. It's like memorizing *TV Guide* rather than watching the show."

The psalms are "the real thing." They are "the show." Little wonder, then, that Jesus himself loved them so much and prayed them so often. In fact, when he was dying, the words of a psalm were on his lips.

How acquainted am I with the psalms? Do any of them speak to me and for me?

✧ God, give me a greater love and appreciation of the psalms.

62. Summer Squash and Snapdragons

I like to think of nature as an unlimited radio station through which God speaks to us every hour, if we will only tune in.
—*George Washington Carver*

Plants are clever. Take summer squash, for instance. If you walk into a garden in the early morning hours, you will see squash plants covered with large yellow blossoms, abuzz with pollinating bees, both honey and bumble. The fascinating thing about these blossoms is this: they are all male. You can recognize them by their straight stems. The female flowers, on the other hand, remain tightly furled above their more puffy stems. No bee, no matter how ambitious, can get into one of them—until later in the day, that is.

An hour or two after the sun has come up, the male flowers are wilted and drooping from the busyness of all those bees. But the female flowers are just beginning to open up. The bees, covered with pollen from the male blossoms, now move on to the fresh female flowers and, presto, fertilization takes place. By opening its blossoms in sequence—first male, then female—the squash plant assures that almost all of its female blossoms will be pollinated. This little trick is one reason summer squash, like zucchini, is so prolific!

Snapdragons have a similar trick. Why do they "snap" when you hold the blossom between your fingers and squeeze? Their character-istic "hinge" serves a purpose. When a bee lands on the lower petal, the flower springs open, exposing the nectar-filled interior. As soon as the bee scurries inside the flower to get some of that nectar, the flower snaps shut, trapping the bee inside. Eventually, the bee will find its way out, of course, but not before it is thoroughly drenched with pollen. Snapdragons "snap" to insure their thorough pollination—which in turn insures that there will be future snapdragons!

Gardener Cass Peterson, reflecting on the cleverness of plants, says, "Plants were dealt a disadvantage in the game of life. They aren't very mobile. They can sometimes throw a seed or send a run-ner over where the soil is better, but for the most part they're stuck where they are. So they make the best of it."

Summer squash and snapdragons are just two examples of plants that have devised clever ways to compensate for a disadvantage, that is, their lack of mobility. Here are two plants that have made the best of it. Is there a lesson in this for us human beings?

What is a disadvantage I have been dealt in the game of life?
How am I trying to make the best of it?

✧ God, help me to make the best of whatever life deals me.

63. On Trembling

Secular people may have made God nonexistent, but we who are religious sometimes make God so ordinary as to be irrelevant. —
Mark William Olson

Writer Mark William Olson raises a good question in his article, "When Hearts Melt Like Wax," *(The Other Side*, March/April 1998). He asks, "Why is it, I wonder, that we modern Christians so seldom tremble?" The ancient Israelites trembled before God on Mount Sinai (Exodus 19:16). The psalmist encouraged his people to tremble: "Tremble before the Lord, all the earth" (Psalm 96:9). Even St. Paul told the early Christians that salvation would be accompanied by trembling: "Work out your salvation with fear and trembling" (Philippians 2:12). Olson continues: "Yet, seldom do I tremble. Is it because trembling is out of fashion, inconsistent with the modern spirit? Or is it because I've let God go out of fashion, closing my eyes and ears to all that is holy?"

Olson's words came to my mind recently when, at the National Gallery of Art, I viewed an exhibition by Lorenzo Lotto, an Italian Renaissance painter. Of the fifty paintings I saw, the one that most caught my fancy was his depiction of the Annunciation. It is unlike any Annunciation I have ever seen. What makes it unique? In most renderings of the scene, Mary is shown calmly accepting the angel's announcement that she will bear the son of God. But in Lotto's Annunciation, Mary looks startled—downright scared to death—at the appearance of the angel. She shrinks away from Gabriel as if she cannot bear the sight of him. Her hands are raised in surprise, her head is tucked down in fear. In other words, Mary is trembling.

God the Father is also shown in the picture not as someone soft and gentle, but as strong and stern. He is pointing both hands directly down at Mary, almost as if zapping her into pregnancy. But my favorite "person" in the picture is Mary's cat. The brown scrawny cat, with its back arched and its teeth exposed, is darting away in terror at these heavenly visitors. I asked about the cat. The woman directing the viewing said that some people see the cat as a symbol of Satan. Then she said, "But I see the cat as an ordinary cat. It's terrified reaction confirms for Mary that these visitors are indeed real and not merely figments of her imagination."

Olson's article and Lotto's painting raise some questions for our reflection. Do we ever tremble before God or have we made God too warm and cuddly? Have we turned God into someone who never threatens or disturbs us? Is God so ordinary as to be irrelevant?

Is there a place for trembling in my relationship with God?

✧ God, help me to tremble before your majesty.

64. The Man with the Barrel

Work in this fundamental sense is not what we do for a living, but what we do with our living. —William Bennett

Today, while sitting in prayer on the third floor porch, I glanced over at the field next door and saw a man rolling a large gray barrel up the hill. The man, wearing jeans, heavy boots, a dull red jacket, and thick brown gloves, was pushing the barrel up toward a television tower perched on top of that hill. I watched him straining: push, push, push! He stopped periodically and, resting the barrel against his leg, stretched his back and measured how far he still had to go. Then bending over again, he continued with his task: push, push, push!

I found myself envying the man. It didn't take me long to figure out why. For here was a human being performing a simple task: get barrel up hill. Granted, I didn't envy the strain of his labor, but I did envy how concrete and clearly defined his task was. I envied too how easy it was for him to measure the progress of his labor. He always knew exactly where he stood, that is, how far he had come and how far he still had to go. And lastly, he was going to know if he had achieved success or not. If he got the barrel up the hill, success; mission accomplished. If he didn't, no success; try again. Or maybe, go and get help.

My feelings of envy arose from the realization that many of the important tasks I am engaged in right now are not that simple, nor that clearly defined. What tasks? Getting an education. Teaching. Writing. The more I thought about it, the more I realized that most of life's really important tasks are far from simple and clear. Take parenting. Take growing in faith. Take praying. Take all loving. Unlike the man with the barrel, we do not always have the satisfaction of knowing exactly where we stand. Nor are we always able to measure our success.

That's where trust comes in. Thomas Merton wrote to a friend who was fretting over his spiritual progress: "Above all, don't be worried about the pace, about what is happening, about what seems to be going on on the surface. Hand that over to God, and believe that below the surface our mind and will and heart are being drawn into a place where God is at work." It takes considerable trust in God to keep plugging away at the task of growing spiritually.

What are some of the important tasks I am currently engaged in that are not simple and clear? What role does trust in God play in my spiritual growth?

✧ Loving God, help me to trust that, below the surface, my mind, will, and heart are being drawn to a place where you are at work.

65. The Delight of Children's Proverbs

A grownup is a child with layers on. —Woody Harrelson

A first-grade teacher brought some well-known proverbs to school one day. She gave each child in her class the first half of the proverb and had them fill in the second half. Since most of the children were unfamiliar with the proverbs, they came up with some rather unique proverbs of their own:

- Better safe than.........punch a fifth grader.
- Strike while the.........bug is close.
- It's always darkest before.........daylight savings time.
- You can lead a horse to water, but.........how?
- Don't bite the hand that.........looks dirty.
- You can't teach an old dog new.........math.

- The pen is mightier than the.........pigs.
- An idle mind is.........the best way to relax.
- Where there's smoke, there's.........pollution.
- Children should be seen and not.........spanked or grounded.
- Cry and.........you have to blow your nose.
- Two's company, three's.........the musketeers.
- When the blind leadeth the blind.........get out of the way.
- A penny saved is.........not much.

The humor in the children's version of these proverbs stems from our familiarity with the original. We know how each proverb is supposed to end (a penny saved is a penny earned), and so we are surprised and we laugh when they end differently (a penny saved is not much.)

Someone has said that God, above all, is a God of surprises. That means there's going to be a lot of laughter in heaven, the place where "supposed to" gives way to God's delightful surprises.

Have I ever experienced a "supposed to" that gave way to a delightful surprise?

✧ God, make me more sensitive to your delightful surprises.

66. Jesus at the Intersection

He is dead and gone, but still he lives—as the living, energetic thought of successive generations, and as the awful motive of a thousand great events. —John Henry Newman

The intersection of Woodward Avenue and 12 Mile Road in Royal Oak, Michigan, is a very busy place. It is where eight lanes of Woodward traffic cross four lanes of 12 Mile traffic. On the northeast corner of that intersection stands a Catholic church, the Shrine of the Little Flower. The church boasts a high tower made of limestone. Carved on the front of that tower is a twenty-eight-foot-tall figure of Jesus hanging on the cross. In the daytime, the figure is clearly visible from any point of the intersection. At night, it is lit for all to see.

Living nearby, I pass through that intersection several times a day. More often than not, I find myself stopped at that intersection. (I'm convinced, when the traffic light there recognizes my car coming, it immediately turns red!) As I sit there waiting for the light to change, I often glance up at that huge crucified Jesus looming over the intersection. I wonder how many other passersby (believers and nonbelievers alike) notice that imposing figure. And if they do, what do they think about it? Here are some of my thoughts.

The first thing that strikes me is the contrast between the stillness of that tower and the busyness of the intersection. There's Jesus hanging motionless and fixed. Here's us, dashing and darting by. To me, that figure of Jesus is (to use T. S. Eliot's phrase) "the still point" of our scurrying. Another contrast that hits me is Jesus' bigness compared to our smallness. His figure dwarfs the cars and trucks that are stopped at the intersection or speeding through it. I find myself asking, "How big is Jesus in my life?" And, "Am I connecting my many activities to this man's single sacrifice on the cross?"

And finally, I have come to think of Jesus as the guardian of that busy intersection. As I pass through it, I sometimes say this little prayer: "Jesus, you are the guardian of all the major and minor intersections of my life! Direct my ways, left or right or straight through. Remind me that you allow U-turns, too."

How am I connecting the busyness of my life with the sacrifice of Jesus on the cross?

✧ Jesus, be the guardian of all the intersections of my life—both major and minor.

67. The Magic of Kevin Kaplowitz

We do not do great things, we do only small things with great love. —Mother Teresa

Kevin Kaplowitz is a fifteen-year-old magician in Los Angeles. When he was only ten, he started putting on magic shows for patients in hospitals and nursing homes. He recalls the first time he entered a burn unit to do a show and was met by the wails of a little girl suffering from third-degree burns. "I made her a balloon animal, and she started smiling and laughing," Kevin said. "I got her to forget her pain."

The tuxedo-clad boy performs card tricks, pulls handkerchiefs out of an empty box, and connects ropes by sleight of hand. He also performs magic at local restaurants and donates the fifteen to twenty dollars an hour he earns to local hospitals and to programs for disadvantaged children. A nurse specialist at one hospital remarked, "We try to give Kevin a twenty-five-dollar gift certificate for a local mall, but he turns around and gives us one hundred dollars for our cancer program."

Where did Kevin learn to help others like this? Probably from watching his mother who volunteers to tutor neighborhood kids, and his older sister Karen who started dancing for hospital patients when she was only four.

The real magic in this story lies not in the tricks that Kevin performs. Rather, it lies in Kevin's sensitivity and generosity, and in the persuasive example of his mother and sister. The artist Vincent van Gogh said to his brother, "I feel that there is nothing more truly artistic than to love people." There is nothing more truly magical, either.

How have others touched me by the magic of their love? How am I doing small things with great love?

✧ Jesus, touch me with the magic of your love today. And help me to touch others with the magic of my sensitivity and generosity.

68. And Jesus Wept

> *(One) cannot heal who has not suffered much,*
> *For only Sorrow sorrow understands;*
> *They will not come for healing at our touch*
> *Who have not seen the scars upon our hands.*
> —Edwin Poteat

Shortly before his own death, Jesus gets word that Lazarus, one of his best friends, is very ill. By the time Jesus gets back to Judaea, he learns that Lazarus has been dead for several days. When Jesus meets Lazarus' sisters, Mary and Martha, and sees their tears, Jesus himself weeps, so much so that observers remark, "See how he loved him" (John 11:36).

The German theologian Karl Rahner, SJ, believed that the words "And Jesus wept" (John 11:35) are perhaps the most significant words in the gospel. Why? Because they demonstrate that it was Jesus' ability to weep and enter into communion with people that permitted him to bring them salvation. In other words, Jesus saved people not by standing outside their experience of pain, but by entering into it. And the entrance fee was his own vulnerability.

We are quick to assume that we help others by being strong: "You cry, I'll hold your hand...you scream, I'll remain calm...you've sinned, but I've been good." Sometimes we do help others in this way, but more often than not, we help them by admitting and even showing our own weakness and powerlessness: "You cry and I'll cry too...you scream, and I'll scream too...you've sinned, and I've sinned too."

Several years ago Father William Buckley, SJ, wrote a letter to his Jesuit brothers who were about to be ordained. In it, he asked them if they were weak enough to be priests. He said: "What do I mean by weakness?...The experience of a peculiar liability to suffering. A profound sense of inability both to do and protect...an inability to secure one's own future...or to ward off shame and suffering."

Describing this way of ministering to others, Julie Collins, a theology teacher at Georgetown Prep, said this: "Like Mary and John standing at the foot of the cross, all we can do is be there, all we can do is weep, all we can do is refuse to run away."

Have others ever ministered to me by just being there, by weeping with me, by refusing to run away? Have I ever ministered to others in this way?

✣ Jesus, help me to minister to others today through my weakness and vulnerability.

69. The Fragility of an Ego

Every major change is a crisis in self-esteem.
—Anonymous

Toward the end of first grade, I got invited to Brucie Pendergeist's birthday party. I was very excited, not because I liked Brucie that much, but because Brucie had a pony. And his invitation clearly stated there would be pony rides at the party. For days, I talked about nothing else but that party—and pony. In my imagination, I saw myself perched high upon that pony, like Dale Evans astride her Buttermilk. When the day finally came, I couldn't wait until eleven o'clock for Mrs. Ratray to drive in with her big blue station wagon and whisk me away to that party—and to that pony.

Sure enough, promptly at eleven, I spotted Mrs. Ratray's station wagon slowly turning into our long gravel driveway, the car packed with a half dozen or so of my first-grade friends. I yelled to my mother, "THEY'RE HERE! I'M GOING! 'BYE!" and flew out the side door. In my excitement, however, I didn't look where I was going. I missed the top step and found myself rolling head over heels down the porch steps—all six of them—and landing in a heap at the bottom. When I looked up, I saw the faces of my friends staring at me from inside the car, their eyes wide with horror and amazement.

Instantly I picked myself up, hobbled back up the steps, ran into the house and into my bedroom, threw myself across my bed, and sobbed and sobbed. I was totally humiliated! Through my tears I announced to my ministering mother, "I'M (sob, sob)...NOT (sob, sob)...GOING (sob, sob)!" I felt I could never face my friends again, not after falling so clumsily and stupidly in front of them.

It took quite some time (and quite some gentleness) for my mother to talk me into going to that party. How she convinced me, I don't remember. But I do remember I was glad she did. For I did get to ride Brucie's pony that day. And I did look just like Dale Evans, too!

That childhood incident taught me an unforgettable lesson: the fragility of an ego. It is as if every person wears this invisible sign around the neck: Fragile ego. Handle with care.

In what ways am I aware of the fragility of my own ego? In what ways am I sensitive to the fragility of the egos of others?

✧ Caring God, help me to be more sensitive to the egos of others today.

70. Encouraging Words

Our words can cut or comfort, hinder or help, harass or heal, injure or inspire.... Each time we speak we deliver our own state of the heart address. —William Arthur Ward

Recently I received a letter from a student I taught over twenty-five years ago. I remember Kathi well: long blonde hair, vivacious, good. In her letter she reminded me how, when I had her in high school, she had wanted to be a nurse "in the worst way," but she always had a hard time in science. She said that one day I told her, "Kathi, it is not always the A students who make the best nurses." She added, "I have always kept that in mind, Sister, and now twenty-some years after graduating from nursing school, I continue to hear your voice."

I was deeply touched by Kathi's letter. I have no recollection of having said those words to her, of course. I have a hard time remembering what I said yesterday, let alone twenty-five years ago! Yet, I am happy that Kathi remembers those words, and I thank God for giving me the grace to say such encouraging words to a young, struggling student.

Kathi's letter led me to reflect on some of the words Jesus said in the gospel that must have encouraged the person or persons to whom they were addressed, words that still retain the power to encourage us as well. Although there are many such words to choose from, I have selected three:

• "Take heart...your sins are forgiven" (Matthew 9:2). Jesus spoke these words to a certain paralytic right before healing him of his paralysis. Jesus speaks these same words to us today. If we truly believed these words, what effect would they have on our demeanor, our attitude, our choices?

• "Whoever does the will of God is my brother and sister and mother" (Mark 3:35). Individuals who are related to famous people often take pride in that fact. They boast, "I'm a direct descendent of Queen Victoria" or "My third cousin once removed is Michael Jordan." But Jesus' words tell us we are directly related to *him*, if we but try to do the will of God. What's more, such kinship with Jesus gives us a justifiable claim to kinship with everyone else who has done the will of God. Just think of the saints we can claim as kin: Mary, Joseph, the Apostles, Francis and Clare, Catherine of Siena, Ignatius, Thomas More, and Elizabeth Seton, just to mention a few.

• "Peace be with you" (John 20:19). These words were the first words of Jesus to his disciples after the resurrection. Recall the scene: the disciples are huddled together, hiding away in an upper room, devastated by the humiliating death of their master. Jesus suddenly appears in their midst and utters these gentle words. How consoled the disciples must have been! Peace, after such an awful storm. Peace, after all that darkness and pain. Peace, after all hope was gone!

Do any of these words of Jesus speak to me today? What other words of Jesus do I find encouraging?

✧ Jesus, speak your encouraging words to me today. And may I in turn speak encouraging words to others.

71. Calls in the Evening

As the evening twilight fades away
The sky is filled with stars, invisible by day.
—Henry Wadsworth Longfellow

In his book, *Get Real About Yourself,* William Larkin tells this story. There once was a cardinal from Venice who was getting on in years. He wrote in his journal that he felt his life was pretty much over. He had been faithful in life and had worked hard, but felt he had not been particularly successful. As far as he was concerned, his life was pretty much behind him. But a few months later, this unknown cardinal from Venice was elected Pope John XXIII.

Pope John XXIII was not the first person to assume that life was over only to learn that it was really just beginning, that God was calling him to start something new. Another individual was the patriarch Abraham. When we meet Abraham in the Book of Genesis, he is over seventy years old. We know virtually nothing about him prior to that time, except that he lived in Ur of Chaldea, took a wife named Sarah, and migrated to Haran in the north. It is almost as if the author of Genesis is saying, "Everything you have ever done in your life pales in significance once you have encountered the living God."

We don't know how God spoke to Abraham in Haran. There is no mention of a burning bush or a thunderbolt from on high. But in whatever way God showed up, it was an intrusion that radically altered the course of Abraham's life. Geographically, his encounter with God caused him to move from Haran to the land of Canaan, not settling in one place but, driven by circumstances, going from Shechem to Bethel to Egypt to Hebron to Damascus to Sodom to…you get the idea. A tracing of Abraham's journey on a map is a maze of crooked and crossing lines, a reminder that sometimes our own journey of life is not a straight line, either.

Abraham's physical journey, however, was but a faint reflection of his spiritual journey: his anguish over his childlessness, his generosity to his nephew Lot, his negotiations with his enemies, his hospitality to strangers, his willingness to sacrifice his only son. How would you begin to graph those?

John XXIII and Abraham: both thought it was time to stop and settle down until God broke into their lives and told them it was time to get up and go.

Have I settled down on my spiritual journey? Or am I ready to get up and go wherever God may be leading me?

✦ Abraham, John, give me some of your daring today.

72. Three Pigeons in the Crosswalk

Animals, like nature, like the whole universe, are filled with God's spirit. —Brother David Steindl-Rast

Someone brought several Labrador retriever puppies to our community's health care facility one day. I wasn't there to witness it, but someone told me it was wonderful. The antics of the puppies made many of the ill and elderly sisters smile. Some sisters asked to hold a puppy. Others stroked them gently while speaking to them sweetly. The puppies gave the sisters something to laugh at, to play with, to talk about, and to take their minds off their pain.

Animals can play a significant role in our spiritual lives. Some people think of animals as angels, that is, as messengers from God. I tend to agree. One afternoon, for example, I was walking through the neighborhood when I spotted three pigeons pecking away on the grass by the side of the street. Suddenly, one of them hopped off the curb and began to walk across the street. The other two followed suit. There they were, three pigeons, all in a row, crossing the street, their heads bobbing back and forth, back and forth. What made the scene particularly funny was this: those pigeons were walking in the crosswalk! It was as if they were intentionally keeping within those yellow painted lines in order to get safely to the other side of the street. I had to smile, and thought, "Go ahead, pigeons. Use our crosswalk. You deserve a safe crossing, too!"

Sometimes our lives can get dull. They can become too predictable, too controlled. But suddenly a chipmunk or lizard comes out of the bushes, a bluebird lands on the fencepost, or a kitten crawls onto our lap—and what happens? The dullness of life disappears. The predictable gives way to the unexpected, the controlled to delightful surprise. The visit of an animal, whether routine or uninvited, can catch our fancy, lift our spirits, and take us out of ourselves. Animals have an amazing capacity to surprise us, and, as Brother David Steindl-Rast has said, "surprise is the only really perfect name for God."

Has an animal ever been a messenger of God for me? If so, how?

✧ God of surprises, help me to be attentive to your messengers I meet today.

73. Why Do We Do Penance?

It's easy to halve the potato where there's love. —Irish proverb

Why do we Christians do penance? Some might say, "We do penance because Jesus did penance." That's true; he did. He worked hard. He gave himself to others. He lived simply and poorly. But Jesus was no killjoy, no sourpuss. For his first miracle (performed at a wedding feast, remember) he changed water into fine wine, not decaffeinated tea. So frequently did Jesus dine at people's houses that his enemies labeled him a glutton.

Others might say, "We do penance because Jesus told us to." Again, that's true. Jesus did tell us to deny ourselves and take up our cross (Mark 8:34). But he never said to do penance for penance's sake. No, there's really only one reason why we do penance: because we love. And genuine love, sooner or later, entails penance. For every time we love someone, we "fast" from our innate tendency toward selfishness. We give up our own agenda or at least modify it to include the agenda or needs of another.

The best kind of penance, therefore, is not the "tacked on" kind. (I've been a grouch all day, but I'll skip dessert at supper.) It isn't the see-how-disciplined-I-can-be kind, either. (I do fifty push-ups every morning before six o'clock, and I never eat more than one piece of popcorn.) No, the best kind of penance grows out of the daily fabric of our lives. It is part and parcel of all we do. Good penance witnesses not so much to our self-control as to our self-giving.

What are some examples of this kind of penance? Being present to people and not preoccupied merely with our own concerns and interests. Being pleasant with people. This means fostering a warm, friendly, and approachable demeanor. Being flexible, that is, being open to new ideas and new ways of doing things. When outsiders observed the early Christians, they did not say, "Look how penitential they are!" But rather, "Look how much they love one another!"

What are some of the penances I do that flow from my love for others? How present, pleasant, and flexible am I?

✤ Jesus, may all my penances be an outgrowth of my love for you and others.

74. The Marching Band

Do not withdraw from community. —Hillel

One summer when I was on retreat, there was a marching band practicing at the high school next door. It was a new band. Consequently, their sharps were flat, their flats were sharp, and their rhythm was off, most of the time. Their band director, a valiant soul, could be heard on his portable microphone yelling things like, "Trumpets, you're flat! Clarinets, you're off! Tuba, you're going the wrong way!" Meanwhile, we retreatants were trying to pray. Some of us, myself included, found ourselves becoming irritated by the band's blatant invasion of our silence and solitude. Once, for example, as we gathered quietly in chapel for Mass, we suddenly heard from the football field next door the unmistakable strains of "Hello, Dolly!"—not exactly the most appropriate entrance hymn for liturgy.

I shared my annoyance with my director, Sister Judy. She sympathized with me and then suggested that I try dialoguing with the marching band in my journal. "Who knows," she said, "the band just might bestow some of its wisdom on you." So I did. Here is part of that dialogue:

Life is like marching in a band. Know this: as long as you are in the band, you will never see the overall pattern of your movements. But that's okay. Take your eight steps this way, your ten steps that way, and mark time if you're asked to. Trust the director who sees the overall design. You will never hear the overall sound of the band either. If you play the trumpet, you will hear mostly trumpet. If you're near the drums, you will hear mostly drums. But trust the director who hears the full band. Follow the director's beat.

Be content to play your part and play it well even if you don't carry the melody. Cherish your instrument: if it's a clarinet, fine; a flute, great; a bass drum, wonderful. Remember: each instrument has a unique contribution to make to the music, even the lowly piccolo. If you find yourself envying another's instrument, just ask yourself: "Who wants a band of all flutes or all tubas?" If you are tempted to be proud of the part you play, remind yourself that it is the harmony of the other instruments that makes you sound so good.

And finally, dare to play all kinds of music. Say not, "I play only Sousa." Try Gershwin, Rodgers and Hammerstein, Mozart even.

What lessons can I learn from a marching band? Are there annoyances in my life from which I can gain wisdom?

✧ God, the leader of my life, help me to follow your beat and direction today.

75. The Disciples of Jesus

The disciples do not come off as recruitment-poster models—flawless, handsome, bigger than life. —Donald Senior, CP

There was nothing unusual about Jesus having disciples. Most wandering preachers of his day had them. But there were several unique features of discipleship with Jesus. First, in Jesus' day one ordinarily became a disciple by choice, which meant the disciple chose the master. With Jesus, however, one became a disciple through a call. Jesus sees the fishermen on the shore and says, "Follow me, and I will make you fish for people" (Matthew 4:19). He sees Matthew at his tax collector's table and says, "Follow me" (Matthew 9:9), and Matthew gets up and follows him. Discipleship with Jesus is dependent upon Jesus' initiative.

Secondly, the call from Jesus is not simply a call to learn a body of knowledge. It is, in the words of Donald Senior, "a call to a relationship with Jesus that never ceases." In addition, the call entails a share in the work of Jesus. Just as Jesus preached, expelled demons, anointed with oil, and cured the sick, his disciples would do the same (Mark 6:12–13). Furthermore, Jesus' disciples share in his style of life as well as his hardships and sufferings.

The status of Jesus' disciples is amazing. They walk with Jesus, enjoy his trust, partake in his mission, and share his power. But there is one more feature of Jesus' disciples that deserves mention: his disciples were incredibly human. Their backgrounds were ordinary, even prosaic. Often, they really did not understand Jesus' message. They were ambitious, vying for places at Jesus' right hand. And, most noteworthy of all, they deserted Jesus in his final hour. But the last word on their discipleship is not their betrayal of Jesus; it is their reconciliation with him after the resurrection. As Senior says, "In the face of the Master they failed, the disciples detected the infinite compassion of God, and they committed this memory to the church."

The first disciples of Jesus both challenge and encourage us. They challenge us to give ourselves wholeheartedly to the person of Jesus and to his mission. And they encourage us to trust in his compassion when we fall short of that ideal.

To what extent can I call myself a disciple of Jesus?

✧ Jesus, help me to follow you as your disciple.

76. The Hard Work of Faith

The love we dream about is tested by the actualities
of this particular person at this particular time.
—John Kavanaugh, SJ

In the movie, *Dead Man Walking*, there is a scene at the end when an angry and grieving father says to Sister Helen, "I wish I had your faith." Sister Helen (played by Susan Sarandon) replies, "It's not faith. I wish it were that simple. It's work!"

That simple declaration is amazingly profound. Faith is work. It is hard work. We tend to think of faith in terms of a gift. Even the new *Catechism of the Catholic Church* says, "Faith is a gift of God, a supernatural virtue infused by (God)" (153). But it is a gift that makes incredible demands upon us—demands upon our time, energy, generosity, and patience. Little wonder when St. Paul encouraged St. Timothy to keep the faith, he used battle imagery: "Wage the good warfare" (1 Timothy 1:18).

But Christian faith is hard work, is warfare, not simply because it is a struggle of good against evil. Says journalist Stephanie Salter, "It is the struggle that comes with Christian territory, the one that is inherent in a philosophy and faith based on the toughest command ever issued: Love one another as I have loved you."

Even the holiest among us can encounter someone who seems impossible to love. It can be someone notorious: the convicted murderer, the serial rapist, the terrorist, the child molester. Or, more often than not, it is someone more ordinary but no less irritating: the old woman next door who talks too much, the child who misbehaves all the time, the teenager who sulks all day, the homeless man who smells bad, the former friend who said such hurtful things.

What enables us to persevere in a faith that demands such love? One thing is this: that we see ourselves in the person we are struggling to love. The old saying, "There but for the grace of God go I," can sound somewhat self-righteous, yet it makes a valid point: that other person and I are far more alike than I sometimes would care to admit. Author Christina Feldman wrote: "'I' and 'you,' 'us' and 'them,' 'winning' and 'losing,' 'victor' and 'vanquished,'—these are no more than the tricks of the mind exiled from the heart." Our faith calls us to see, in every face before us, the resemblance to our own face.

What are some of the struggles I experience in trying to live out my faith? What helps me to love people who are difficult to love?

✧ Jesus, help me to persevere in living your commandment of love today.

77. Manners

There is no outward sign of true courtesy that does not rest on a deep moral foundation. —Johann Wolfgang von Goethe

Several years ago, columnist Mike Royko devoted a column to jerks. He began by defining what a jerk is: "Jerks are those who seem unaware that others exist. Or, if they are aware, they just don't care." According to Royko, jerks think they are the center of the universe. Royko went on to say that there are minor jerks and major jerks. When driving, we see both kinds. Minor jerks tailgate, lane hop, and babble on their car phones while straddling two lanes. Major jerks speed recklessly, drive while intoxicated, and engage in acts of road rage.

Royko's rather humorous column led me to do some serious thinking. I wondered: aren't jerks essentially people who have no manners? After all, a good definition of polite people is this: they are individuals who are aware that others exist, and who care about them. In other words, polite people know they are not the center of the universe. They demonstrate this every time they hold open a door for someone, use a handkerchief when sneezing, refrain from talking during a movie, and drive responsibly.

Unfortunately, we don't hear too much about manners these days—my personal love for Miss Manners notwithstanding. With our emphasis on individual freedom and wholesale tolerance, manners can somehow seem restrictive or unnecessary. It is interesting to note, however, that much of what we think of as politeness is rooted in fundamental Judeo-Christian concepts. The *New Emily Post's Etiquette,* by Elizabeth Post, puts it this way: "All good manners are based on thoughtfulness of others, and if everyone lived by the Golden Rule—'Do unto others as you would have others do unto you'—there would be no bad manners in the world."

Whether I pour my cup of tea first or whether I pour yours first has few, if any, cosmic ramifications. But the tiny, numerous courtesies of everyday living are vital because of the moral foundation upon which they rest. With every polite deed, we are saying to another, "You are important. And I care about you." And such an attitude can have cosmic ramifications.

How polite and courteous am I? Do I see the connection between politeness and my faith?

✧ Jesus, make me more mindful of others today.

78. The White-Haired Army of Believers

Perseverance is the greatest of all teachers.
—Arabian Proverb

Sometimes I think the only reason our world has not been engulfed in fiery perdition long ago is due to the white-haired army of believers who attend Mass every day. I am sure you know who I mean, for every parish has them—those elderly women and men (definitely more women than men) whom you see every morning shuffling into our churches for daily Mass. Despite their arthritis, their bent backs, their canes and walkers, these men and women are on time for Mass. In fact, they are usually early. If Mass is at 8:30 a.m., they're there at 8:00 a.m. so they have time to light their candles (if the church still has any), say the stations (if the church still has any), and pray their rosaries (often aloud and together).

I admire these churchgoing senior citizens. They give the definite impression they are at home in God's house. They should be, for they have been coming to church faithfully for many, many years. Often their faith has been the one constant in their lives, lives characterized by periodic misfortunes, catastrophic change, and personal tragedies. Most have raised families, sometimes large ones. They have guided those families through depression, recession, and (sometimes the most difficult of all) economic prosperity.

Some have lived to see their children's faith grow lukewarm—the same faith they themselves struggled so hard to keep bright and burning—and their grandchildren's faith grow ice cold. Yet despite their heartache, confusion, and pain, these white-haired believers continue to pray. They pray for their spouses and for their friends, many of whom are dead. They pray for their children, their grandchildren, and great-grandchildren. And they pray for the world, a world too ready to ignore them, one that grows more alien to them with each new advance in technology.

We who call ourselves believers can learn much from our senior citizens. We can learn about the few eternal values worth building a life upon: faith, family, love, honesty, friendship, and prayer. We can learn what it means to be faithful, not just for today but for a lifetime. And, most of all, we can learn what it means to believe in a God who is, as St. Augustine said, "ever ancient and ever new."

Are there any senior citizens in my life that inspire me? If so, in what way?

✢ God, help me to persevere in my faith.

79. Spilled Milk

The power is knowing that you can, but you don't.
—Juliet Alicia Jarvis

Retreat director and writer Sister Jose Hobday tells this story from her childhood. Where she grew up in the Southwest, certain places did not serve Native Americans. One day Jose and her mother, a Native American, stopped into a restaurant for something to drink. Her mother ordered a cup of coffee and she a glass of milk. The waitress brought the glass of milk, but did not bring the coffee.

When Jose saw the waitress standing idly by the cash register, she got up, went over to her, and said, "You forgot my mother's coffee." But the waitress didn't move. When Jose got back to the booth, her mother said softly, "Jo, I think this is one of those places that doesn't serve Indian people." Jose was shocked. How could they not serve her mother? She became furious.

Then her mother suggested they get up and leave. As they did, Jose took her glass of milk and slowly poured it all over the booth— the seats, the table, the floor. She said, "I remember thinking, if they weren't going to serve my mother, they were going to remember they didn't serve her. I was going to give them a cleanup job they would not forget." Her mother didn't say anything to her as she emptied the glass, but when she was finished her mother said, "Well now, Jo, you have proven yourself to be just as stupid as they are." Says Sister Jose, "My mother's response taught me this: Even when you feel you are justified, don't respond in kind when violence has been done to you."

When we think of acts of violence, we usually think of fist fights, stabbings, shootings, and bombings. But there are other more subtle acts of violence, too: slamming doors, calling someone a jerk, driving recklessly, talking down to a person, harboring racist or sexist thoughts, refusing to speak to someone. Jesus told us, "When someone strikes you on your right cheek, turn the other one to him as well" (Matthew 5:39). We hear those words and are tempted to say, "You're kidding, right?" And Jesus replies, "No. I'm not kidding."

Are there any traces of violence and revenge in my attitudes and actions? What does Jesus' own life and death teach me about violence?

✧ Jesus, cleanse me of all violent attitudes and actions.

80. Meeting the Real Jesus

We arrive at truth, not by reason alone, but also by the heart. —Blaise Pascal

Charlie Chaplin once entered a Charlie Chaplin look-alike contest in Monte Carlo. Imagine his surprise when he came in third! This anecdote got me to wondering: if Jesus returned to the earth and entered a Jesus look-alike contest, would he win? Or would he come in third or tenth or seventeenth? In other words, who is Jesus, really? Perhaps the more important question is this: who is Jesus, really, *for me?*

Is Jesus my friend, that is, someone with whom I share an intimate relationship? Do I converse with Jesus on a regular basis? Do I share my hopes and fears, my joys and sorrows with Jesus as I do with my closest friends? Do I ponder his words and example as I find them in Scripture? Do I lean on him in tough times?

Is Jesus my savior? In his book, *Vision 2000*, Mark Link, SJ, tells of a navy helicopter pilot who was telling his parents about helicopters. He said that as complicated as helicopters are, their rotors are held in place by a single hexagonal bolt. He added, "It's called a Jesus nut!" A question we might want to ask ourselves is this: is Jesus the one who holds my life together?

Another way to discover who Jesus is for us is to learn who Jesus is for others. Their thoughts and feelings can enrich our own experience.

- Jesus is not an aspirin tablet. Jesus is a lover who holds us in a lover's embrace as we travel this headache called life. (Jack Pantaleo)

- Christ is my music, my horizon, my sea, and my green woods. (Miriam Pollard, OCSO)

- Thou are the Way
Hadst Thou been nothing but the goal,

I cannot say
If Thou hadst ever met my soul. (Alice Meynell)

Who is Jesus, really, for me?

✧ Jesus, help me to know the real you.

81. Creativity: Faith's Dancing Partner

What does God do all day long? God gives birth.
—Meister Eckhart

The eighteenth-century poet William Blake said that imagination is "the divine body in everyone." It might seem strange that he so readily connects imagination with the divine, yet there is certainly scriptural evidence to support such a linkage. From the very first pages of the Bible, for example, God is shown as one who is extremely imaginative and creative. God utters "Let there be..." and brings everything—every thing—into being, from the sun to salamanders, from oceans to otters, from the moon to marigolds. When God finally gets around to creating Adam and Eve on the sixth day of creation, God decides to do something even more spectacular: to fashion these humans in God's own image and likeness. Based on what God did those first five days, we can logically assume that a significant component of that image and likeness to God was imagination or creativity.

In his book, *Wrestling the Light*, poet Ted Loder says that imagination or creativity is "a dancing partner of faith." We might ask, in what ways are faith and creativity partners? First, both faith and creativity demand courage. Interestingly, Rollo May's famous book on creativity is even entitled *The Courage to Create*. The creative person must not be afraid to go against the current tide or to threaten the acceptable norm. So, too, must the person of faith.

Faith and creativity are partners because they also require a certain asceticism. Both artists and believers, for example, must learn to befriend solitude. Just as no one can create for us, so too no one can live our faith for us. The ascetical dimension is also present in the specific limitations that are placed upon the artist and the believer by the materials with which they work. The writer, for example, creates within the bounds of language; the sculptor within the constraints of marble and stone. Similarly, our faith too is always exercised within limitations—the limitations of our specific time, circumstances, and personhood.

And finally, both creativity and faith require perseverance. Artists don't create only when they feel like it. Often they must work in spite of fatigue, mistakes, and natural disinclination. Similarly, believers are faithful to prayer and other religious practices in spite of periodic discouragement, setbacks, and doubt.

How's my creativity lately? Have I ever experienced the linkage between creativity and faith?

✧ God of infinite creativity, remind me today that I am fashioned in your image and likeness.

82. On Stories

The universe is made of stories, not atoms. —Muriel Rukeyser

Recently I received a letter from a woman named Margaret who had just finished reading one of my short stories, a rather sad story about two widows. Margaret said she read the story that morning as she was eating breakfast. She wrote, "There I am reading your story and all of a sudden, I'm crying—big tears rolling down my cheeks, into my mouth, and almost into my cereal bowl!" She admitted she couldn't explain why this story had moved her so much. "Probably because it was about human tenderness and love and vulnerability— all of which I needed to remember in the midst of my days of being too busy and too torn by daily struggles and weighty (and not-so-weighty) decisions." She concluded her letter with, "Your story woke something up in me. Thank you. Thank you."

Needless to say, I was deeply touched to think that a story of mine could have had such an impact on someone. Yet I, for one, have never underestimated the power of narrative, for I know from personal experience how often I have been "awakened" by a good story.

John Shea, who has written more than his share of good stories, says this: "Storytelling has a power of involvement and appreciation that mere noting of patterns or talking about experiences analytically does not have." Don't our ears perk up, for example, when the homilist says something like, "A funny thing happened to me on the way to church this morning"? As humans, we seem more drawn to stories than to theological treatises.

Jesus told stories. Lots of them; lots of good ones. He invited us, for example, to slip into the sandals of a man on the road to Jericho or a woman searching frantically for a lost and precious coin, and by doing so, to broaden our perspective, to deepen our own experience, and to discover hidden meaning in the everyday occurrences of our lives. Jesus knew, good theology is best transmitted through good stories. Or, as the writer Sam Keen said, "Story telling...is functionally equivalent to believing in God."

What are some of my favorite stories? Why do I like these stories so much? Do any of them help "awaken" me to ultimate meaning, to belief in God?

✧ God, the origin of all stories, help me to come closer to you through the stories I hear and tell today.

83. Work: A Worthwhile Investment

Work is not a four letter word. —Melannie Svoboda, SND

When I listen to the radio on Monday mornings, I hear things like this: "Well, it's Monday. The beginning of the week! Too bad! We've got four whole days until the weekend! It's tough, but hang in there!" On Wednesdays: "Well, today's Wednesday. Two days down and two to go! Look at the bright side: we're halfway to the weekend!" And on Friday, the familiar, "Thank God it's Friday!" When I hear things like this, I get a little annoyed. The announcers make it sound as if the only thing worth living for is the weekend! Now don't get me wrong, I like weekends too. I appreciate time off. I look forward to vacations. But I also like to work.

I like to work. Even as I typed that sentence I felt a little strange. How many people today openly admit they like to work—even if they do? (I am not including the so-called workaholics, mind you, who not so much *like* to work as that they are *addicted* to work. Big difference.) I, for one, agree with Rumer Godden, who said, "I never understood why hard work is supposed to be pitiable.... You get tired, of course...but the struggle, the challenge, the feeling of being extended as you never thought you could be, is fulfilling and deeply, deeply satisfying."

One reason we sometimes get so bogged down with work is this: we fail to connect what we do with the people for whom we do it. I was attending a meeting in Rome once when our congregation's top secretary gave a little talk on the work she does. Now here's a woman who sits by herself at a desk all day and (as some would say) shuffles papers. But she shared with us a little practice she devised. Whenever she works on the records of a particular sister, she gets out a photo of that sister and lays it on her desk. "While I'm working on those papers," she said, "I glance at the picture every now and then. It reminds me that I'm doing this work for a particular person." What a wonderful little practice: to keep before us the image of the individuals for whom we are working: our families, our patients, our students, our clients—even our God!

In *The Book of Virtues*, William Bennett says that the opposite of work is not leisure, play, or having fun. It is idleness, which he defines as "not investing ourselves in anything." Work, then, is meaningful and worthwhile precisely when it is an investment of ourselves in others. And another name for such an investment is love.

What is my attitude toward my work? Do I see it as an investment in others?

✧ God, who is always working for my salvation, help me to see my work as a way of loving others—and you!

84. Sister Mary David

"Good" is the movement in the direction of home.
—Martin Buber

I first met Sister Mary David Horan when I was a freshman in high school. I had her for homeroom, religion, and Latin. She was an excellent teacher, lively, demanding, and gentle. I was immediately drawn to her. After school I found myself hanging around her room, under the pretext of helping her wash the boards, but in reality I was basking in her Irish wit and in the attention she lavished upon me. When I became a senior and was struggling with whether to become a nun or not, Sister David was the person I sought out for advice and encouragement. To this day I attribute my precious religious vocation largely to her influence.

Sister David loved teaching. She once said she saw teaching as "an opportunity to bring God's goodness to young people." In her early years she taught elementary school. But later she taught both high school and college. In her final years before retirement, she taught and tutored students who were academically challenged. Said a colleague, "Sister had a gift for making these students feel special and for empowering them to do their best."

Sister David loved words. Her favorite word was "hydraulic" which she was fond of saying over and over again, delighting in its sound. She was an expert in grammar, punctuation, and correct usage. For a time, she served as a proofreader for our community's religious textbook series. Even in her last years when she was a patient in our health care facility, she always had a novel and a crossword puzzle within arm's reach.

Illness and old age were not easy for Sister David to accept. Among friends she sometimes raged against her increasing incapacity, but then would add, "But even in my illness I have much to be grateful for, like time to pray for people." Even to the end, she managed to hang on to her sense of humor. As she lay dying, one visiting sister asked, "How are you, Sister David?" She replied dryly, "Now that is a stupid question!" On her night stand, she had a calendar with a word and definition for every day of the year. On the day she entered eternity, the calendar said "mesmerize," defined as "to hold spellbound."

We long for role models only to find ourselves disappointed by elected officials, prominent businessmen, and professional athletes who cheat, steal, and act like spoiled children. But I'm convinced that there are role models all around us, too numerous to count, too humble to draw much attention: real role models, like Sister David.

Who has been a role model for me? Why?

✧ God, I thank you for the role models you have given me, especially for_____.

85. You Needed Me

I used to ask God to help me. Then I asked if I might help God.
—Hudson Taylor

Recently I went to an Anne Murray concert with a friend. About halfway through the concert, Murray announced she was about to sing her favorite of the 300 songs she has recorded. With that, she began the familiar strains of "You Needed Me." I was thrilled, for that's one of my favorite songs, too. In fact, I often use it during retreats. But before I play the song for a group, I first say something like this, "Pretend that you are singing these words to God." In other words, say to God, "You needed me."

Now, out there somewhere is a theologian who is going to read what I have just written and is going to protest, "No! That's heresy! God does not need me! God does not need you! God does not need anybody!" Strictly speaking, that's true. But in another sense, it's not true. God does need me, and you, and everybody.

Jesus—who was, after all, God incarnate—needed people, a fact he made little attempt to hide. When Jesus strolls along the sea of Galilee and calls those fishermen to be his first disciples, what else is he doing but admitting, "I need you"? When, after a hectic road tour, he stops in to visit Mary, Martha, and Lazarus in Bethany, what else is he doing but confessing, "I need the three of you"? When he asks Peter, James, and John to go with him into the garden of Gethsemane and pray with him, isn't he really telling them, "I need you"? And, after the resurrection, when he tells his disciples to go and proclaim the good news to the ends of the earth, he is really crying out in capital letters, *"I need you!"*

On a natural level it feels good to be needed by someone—a spouse, a child, a friend, a student, a client. How much greater it should make us feel to know we are needed by Almighty God! Yes, God needs us to raise children, teach math, cook meals, do research, cure patients, preach sermons, plant tulips, write books, compose songs, scrub floors. At the end of the day, as we crawl into bed after serving God through serving other people, our final prayer could be, "Thank you, God, for needing me!"

How does God need me? Who else needs me?

✧ Thank you, God, for needing me!

86. The Women in My Kitchen

The most important decision we can make in life is choosing our ancestors. —Anonymous

Whenever I make dumplings, a group of women suddenly shows up in my kitchen: my female ancestors. Although I cannot see them, I know they are with me, waiting and watching. My mother is with me, for she is the one who gave me the dumpling recipe in the first place. Grandma's there, too, for she is the one who, as a young girl, carried the recipe with her from Bohemia to Cleveland and handed it down to my mother. My great-grandmother, whom I never met, is there too, and her mother and her mother and so on. Although my kitchen is tiny, I know they are all there, hovering over my shoulder, checking to see if I am doing things right, and smiling.

The recipe for dumplings is simple: flour, salt, baking powder, potatoes, eggs, milk. In times past, potatoes were sometimes hard to come by, so the recipe learned to get along without them, if necessary. Despite the recipe's simplicity, however, making good dumplings is still an art, dependent on a whole set of rules. Make sure the eggs are fresh. Don't use skim milk. Be sure to cool the potatoes completely after you mash them. The water must really be boiling. Keep the dumplings covered. Leave them in for ten minutes on each side, no more, no less.

Sometimes dumplings don't turn out right even when you obey all the rules; they are too heavy or too dry. Maybe you handled the dough too much or the kitchen was too humid. Whatever the cause, I never get too upset when my dumplings aren't perfect, for I remember that my mother's weren't always perfect either. If they weren't, she would just say, "You can never tell about dumplings..." and her voice would trail off. That was probably something she heard her own mother say when her dumplings didn't turn out right either.

But most times my dumplings do turn out right. They are light and fluffy and moist. When this happens, I rejoice—not in my own skill, but in the fact that all the variables came together for me. And I know the women in my kitchen are pleased, too. I sense they are smiling at each other. I feel their invisible pats on my shoulder. For they know that their recipe for dumplings, a recipe that sustained them in good times and bad, lives on, sustaining me!

Our faith is a lot like a treasured family recipe, not so?

In what ways is our faith like a treasured family recipe?

✧ God, I thank you for my ancestors in the faith. And I ask you to bless my descendants in the faith.

87. Thou Shalt Lighten Up

Time spent laughing is time spent with the gods.
—Japanese proverb

Sometimes I think we need an eleventh commandment: thou shalt lighten up. I might be wrong, but I think it's getting harder to hang on to our sense of humor. Maybe we know too much about our world. On any given day, for example, we know that a baby was brutally murdered in New York, there was an earthquake in Outer Mongolia, and a bomb exploded in Sri Lanka. Maybe we know too much about people: this elected official cheated on his wife, this police chief is a racist, and that banker was just convicted of embezzlement. And maybe we know too much about the church, too. That priest was unfaithful, those radicals are at odds with those conservatives, and the latest polls reveal some disturbing trends.

In such a world, keeping a sense of humor is not easy. And so I'm devoting this meditation to a few anecdotes and jokes which I hope will lighten up your day:

• Abraham Lincoln once told a waiter, "If this is coffee, please bring me some tea. But if this is tea, please bring me some coffee."

• A little girl said to her father after Sunday school, "Our teacher must be Jesus' grandmother 'cause she talks about him all the time."

• A cartoon showed a man dining at a fancy restaurant. Sitting across from him was a big stuffed teddy bear. Said the man to the waiter, "My last relationship was too complicated."

• First man: "How's your wife?"
Second man: "Compared to what?"

• Comedian Dan Spencer says: "On cable TV they have a weather channel with twenty-four hours of weather. We had something like that where I grew up. We called it a window."

• Anyone who thinks old age is golden must not have had a very exciting youth. (Marguerite Whiteley May)

• A man was glancing at the cover of a swimsuit issue of a magazine that showed a woman in a skimpy bikini. Disturbed, his wife said, "That's shameful! If I looked like that I wouldn't leave the house!" Her husband replied, "Honey, if you looked like that, *I* wouldn't leave the house!"

How's my sense of humor these days? How can I lighten up?

✧ God, keep me laughing.

88. Sacred Ambiguity

There is much at stake when belief and doubt go to the crucible;
despair might emerge; but with luck, faith and hope appear.
—*Kathleen Norris*

In my book, *Traits of a Healthy Spirituality*, I said that one of the traits of a healthy spirituality is that we can live graciously with a certain amount of ambiguity in our lives. Today I would add: and with a certain amount of ambiguity *in our faith.*

Kathleen Norris, poet and author of *Amazing Grace, Dakota,* and *The Cloister Walk*, tells the story of her own religious conversion, a conversion she partly attributes to her contact with a Benedictine Abbey. One day she visited the abbey and eventually began attending their liturgy of the hours. Although she was deeply moved by the prayer and the obvious faith of the monks, Norris felt her own personal doubts "were spectacular obstacles to faith." She confided this to an elderly monk who told her that doubt was "merely the seed of faith, a sign that faith is alive and ready to grow."

His words encouraged Norris, and she began to attend church. At first she felt as if she didn't belong with the rest of the believers. Only gradually did she realize that we worship not simply because we are believers, but because we wish to become believers. She said, "Worship itself thus became the major instrument of my conversion."

Religious belief is not a once-and-for-all kind of thing. It doesn't mean we have all the answers or that we have a full grip on truth. Faith is a relationship, ever changing and growing. Norris says that religious belief became for her "like a deep friendship or a marriage, something that I could plunge into, not knowing exactly what I was doing or what would be demanded of me in the long run."

When, as believers, we find ourselves up against doubt and ambiguity, perhaps we can say what the father of the young demoniac said to Jesus, "I do believe, help my unbelief!" (Mark 9:24).

What are some of the ambiguities of my faith that I have struggled with in the past or am struggling with now? Do I believe that my doubts can be the seed of faith?

✧ Jesus, I do believe, help my unbelief!

89. Taking Time to Really See

Nobody sees a flower, really—it is so small—we haven't the time,
and to see takes time. —Georgia O'Keeffe

The popular spiritual writer Sister Joyce Rupp, OSM, asks people this question: "When did you last notice your hands?" She then encourages people to spend a few minutes looking at their hands. You might want to do that right now. Notice, for example, how your hands hold this book for you, and how you can turn the pages with them. Look at the tops of your hands. Notice the veins, the joints, the fingernails. Flex your fingers slowly. If they all still work, isn't it incredible? Then turn your hands over and look at your palms. Study the lines, feel the texture of your skin. Be aware of all your hands do for you in a given day: how they help you get up from a chair, enable you to write, comb your hair for you, carry things, reach out, and open doors. Rupp concludes by saying, "Hands are wonderful gifts. It is too easy for us to take our hands for granted until they become arthritic or succumb to some other physical ailment."

It is too easy for us to take not only our hands for granted, but everything for granted: our right knee, the big toe on our left foot, our eyelashes, our liver, our heart. In Betty Smith's book, *A Tree Grows in Brooklyn,* we read: "Look at everything as though you were seeing it either for the first time or last time. Then your time on earth will be filled with joy." There's much wisdom in that.

If you knew, for example, that tonight was going to be the last sunset you would ever see, wouldn't you take the time and effort to watch it? Or if you had never heard a flute before, wouldn't you be enchanted by its strains? Or if this dandelion was the last dandelion you were ever going to see, wouldn't you appreciate it? (I know, I know, if your lawn is filled with them, you might find it hard to imagine you could ever appreciate a dandelion! But years ago, I lived with a Sister from India who, during her first spring in the States, came running into the convent with a fist full of dandelions, excited to show me the beautiful little flowers she had found and eager to know if I knew their name.)

Just as we can take our hands for granted, we can take Scripture for granted, too. We can say, "I've heard that story a million times already." Or, "I know what Jesus is going to say here." It might prove beneficial to stop and pretend we have never heard this passage before. Perhaps by doing so, we may hear it in a brand new way. In fact, we may actually hear it for the very first time.

What am I taking for granted in my life right now? Pretend I am seeing it for the first or last time.

✧ God, help me to take none of your gifts for granted.

90. Asking Jesus for Help

Jesus seems highly allergic to perfect people.... He gets along best with the broken and neurotic. —Jack Pantaleo

Once when I was driving to work, I saw a man walking his two dogs, both golden retrievers. As I got closer, I noticed something unusual. The man had only one leash in his hand. The leash to the second dog was in the mouth of the first dog! I smiled, for it was the first time I had ever seen one dog taking another dog for a walk. Later I thought: that man certainly knows how to delegate authority! He knows how to get help when he needs it.

Some of us, myself included, find it hard to ask others for help. We have taken to heart the rugged individualism characteristic of many of the early European settlers in this country. We think or say things like, "That's okay, I'll do it myself." Or, "No problem. I can handle it." So independent are we, so self-sufficient, our theme song could very well be, "I Did It My Way...and All By Myself!"

There is certainly a place in our lives for responsibility and independence. But there is also a place for asking for help and for admitting our need for others—especially God. If we find it difficult to ask God for help, we can take encouragement from the gospels, for they show a wide range of individuals readily coming to Jesus and asking him for help. In fact, if there is one quality Jesus possessed in abundance it was approachability. He never refused anyone who came to him. On the contrary, he was quick to respond to their needs. "Lord, my servant is dying" (Matthew 8:6). "Lord, make me clean" (Luke

5:12). "Master, my little girl is sick" (Luke 8:42). "Son of David, have pity on me" (Mark 10:48). "Master, I want to see" (Mark 10:51).

Sometimes the best prayer petitions are the shortest ones. We need not approach Jesus with a three-page outline of our current needs or a convoluted speech requesting a specific item. At times, we may not even have a clear awareness of what exactly we need. But that's okay. At such times we can borrow the words of those who have gone before us, those who laid their needs at Jesus' feet with a few succinct words: Lord, have pity on me…cleanse me…heal me…make me see.

Do I really believe that Jesus is approachable? Do I readily ask him for help?

✦ Jesus, help me!

91. Have I Been Good to You Today?

The best way to know God is to be like God.
—St. Gregory of Nyssa

A friend told me this story about her grandmother, Rosie, a woman who was widowed after fifty years of marriage. It seems Rosie was always upbeat and cheerful. One day, my friend asked her grandmother how she managed to keep such a positive attitude even though her life had not been particularly easy. Her grandmother replied, "Your grandfather loved me very much. Every night before going to sleep he used to ask me, 'Have I been good to you today, Rosie?' Some days it was easy for me to say yes. But other days, when we had had an argument or I was mad at him, it was hard for me to say yes. But I always knew how much he still loved me when he asked me that question." Even though her husband had been dead for several years, the memory of his love continued to keep Rosie optimistic.

The story impressed me, for it demonstrated once again the incontrovertible link between knowing we are loved and retaining a positive attitude toward life, regardless of the difficult circumstances in which we may find ourselves. In addition, the story shows the sustaining power of love. Even after death it can continue to influence, direct, and console.

The story also gave me an idea for my own prayer before going to sleep. Sometimes when I crawl into bed, I pretend I hear God saying to me, "Have I been good to you today, Melannie?" It is one way for me to become more aware of the obvious and subtle blessings I have received from God throughout the day. Some nights, it's easy for me to say "Yes, God. You've been good to me. Very good to me." And I effortlessly rattle off some of God's blessings: a moment of consolation, a new insight, a small accomplishment, an experience of intimacy, a good deed. But on other nights, it's hard for me to say yes: when I'm upset at the way something has turned out, or I'm hurt by God's apparent lack of interest in my life, or I'm mad at God's seeming absence in our world. Sometimes, I answer a stubborn, "No, God! You have not been good to me," and turn away and pout.

I, for one, think it's perfectly all right to pout with God. In fact, it's all right to get really mad at God sometimes. At least then we're relating to God as we would relate to a real person. Being mad at God can also be an important stage in developing a closer relationship with God, a step toward greater trust in God even when life doesn't make any sense to us.

I will hear God say to me, "Have I been good to you today?" What is my answer and why?

✧ God, help me to become more aware of all the ways you are good to me today.

92. Seeking God

You will eventually find God whether you want to or not.
—*Words that Carl Jung had chiseled on the lintel of his door*

If there's one thing Scripture tells us to do it is this: "Seek!" In the book of Deuteronomy we read: "You shall seek the Lord, your God; and you shall indeed find him" (Deuteronomy 4:29). Similarly, the psalms talk a lot about seeking. "Seek to serve the Lord constantly"

(Psalm 105:4). And, "One thing I ask of the Lord; this I seek: to dwell in the house of the Lord all the days of my life" (Psalm 27:4). The prophets, too, exhort their people to seek. Isaiah, for example, says, "Seek the Lord while he may be found" (Isaiah 55:6). And Jeremiah puts these words on God's lips, "When you seek me with all your heart, you will find me with you" (Jeremiah 29:13).

Jesus himself told us to be seekers: "Seek and you shall find" (Matthew 7:7). And again, "Seek first the kingdom of God" (Luke 12:31). It is a theme found throughout the writings of Paul as well: "If then you were raised with Christ, seek what is above" (Colossians 3:1).

A question we might want to ask ourselves on a regular basis is this: are we seekers? If so, what or whom are we seeking? We might answer that ultimately, of course, we seek God. But where do we seek God? If we seek God in silence and solitude, do we also seek God in noise and crowds? If we seek God in church, do we also seek God in our home, at work, at a soup kitchen, in the nursing home? If we seek God in prayer, do we also seek God in service? In their book *Compassion*, McNeil, Morrison, and Nouwen write, "Service is an expression of the search for God and not just of the desire to bring about social change."

Do we seek God by seeking to change structures and institutions that are basically unjust? That certainly is important and praiseworthy, as long as we simultaneously seek to change ourselves. For as Bishop Oscar Romero said before he was martyred, "We should not just seek changes in structures, because new structures are worth nothing when there are no new people to manage them and live in them."

Jesus' parables are all about seeking: seeking for pearls, lost coins, lost sheep, a net full of fish, and a father's forgiveness. They are about passion and desire. Obviously, then, a measure of the healthiness of our faith is whether we are still seeking—passionately—to become a better person, to fashion a better world, and to find the living God.

What or whom am I seeking in my life?

✦ God, help me to seek you for I know and believe that you are seeking me.

93. Irish Wisdom

A friend's eye is the best mirror. —*Irish proverb*

I am not Irish. But then again, neither was St. Patrick. But I do have many good friends who are Irish. (So did St. Patrick.) As a tribute to them, I will now share a few of the Irish proverbs I have collected over the years. I'll list them in the order in which I personally like them, saving the best till last:

10. Better a mule that carries you than a fine horse that throws you.

9. If a man fools me once, shame on him.
   If he fools me twice, shame on me.

8. Many a shabby colt makes a fine horse.

7. Be nice to them on the way up. You might meet them on the way down.

6. A good laugh and a long sleep are the two best cures.

5. You've got to do your own growing, no matter how tall your grandfather was.

4. It's as foolish to let a fool kiss you as it is to let a kiss fool you.

3. Your feet will bring you to where your heart is.

2. Don't see all you see, don't hear all you hear.

1. The church is near,
   but the road is icy;
   the tavern is far,
   but I'll walk very carefully.

Do any of these proverbs resonate with me and my experience? If so, which and why?

✧ God, let me share in your wisdom today.

94. Excellence

Excellence is never an accident. —Anonymous

Recently I read an article on architects. In it, the author was trying to learn what distinguished the really good architects from the mediocre ones. Her conclusion? It was not the fact that good architects did things right the first time. No, it was their "willingness to revise, rework, redo."

Isn't this what determines excellence in almost any field, whether architecture or acting, music or cooking, literature or athletics? In general, people are not born excellent; they become excellent largely through their willingness to work hard at what they do. The great Michelangelo once said to someone who envied his work, "If you knew how hard I worked at this, you might not think it was so wonderful." Similarly, a woman once said to the great violinist Fritz Kreisler after a recital, "I'd give my life to play as beautifully as you!" Kreisler replied, "Madam, I have!"

In a way, we are all architects—architects of ourselves. Jesus referred to himself as a building when he said to the religious leaders, "Destroy this temple and in three days I will raise it up" (John 2:19). And St. Paul posed this question for the Corinthians, "Do you not know that you are the temple of God, and that the Spirit of God dwells in you?" (1 Corinthians 3:16). We are all fashioning ourselves into a temple from the materials life sets before us. How hard are we willing to work at this fashioning? Are we prepared to revise, rework, redo? Are we eager to settle for nothing less than the best?

Jesus encourages revisions. He continuously calls us to conversion. His call is nothing less than the call to revise our behavior, to rework our attitude, to redo our priorities. In the spiritual life, as in most other endeavors, it is never too late to make changes. It is never too late to strive for excellence.

Is there anything in my life that I am called to revise, rework, redo?

✧ Jesus, give me the patience and the strength to strive for excellence in my life today.

95. Sorrow and Loss

Where there is sorrow there is holy ground.
—*Oscar Wilde*

Years ago I taught a brilliant young girl named Patti. Patti had a pet rabbit whom she loved dearly. He had only one ear, so she creatively dubbed him Malchus after the man whose ear Peter chopped off in the garden of Gethsemane. Patti loved this rabbit and talked about him often. One day, Patti didn't come to school. This was unusual, for she never missed a day. The next day she came in and explained the reason for her absence: Malchus had died. So distraught was she over finding him dead that morning that she had decided to stay home for the day, knowing she would never be able to concentrate in school. Now some might think her reaction was a little extreme. After all, it was only a rabbit. And yet I, who had numerous pets while I was growing up on the farm, could understand her actions. The pain of loss is hard to bear no matter what we lose, a rabbit or a dog, good health or a reputation, a job or a friend.

Jesus was sensitive to loss. When he chanced upon the widow of Naim burying her only son, he was so moved by the scene that he spontaneously raised the young man to life again without even being asked. (It is comforting to know that even Jesus could be guilty of impulsiveness.) When he gets word of the death of John the Baptist, he goes off by himself to mourn, giving us only a glimpse of what that loss must have meant to him. Jesus was sympathetic to the losses of others. He knew, for example, what it meant for a shepherd to lose a sheep, a woman to lose a coin, a farmer to lose his crop, a father to lose his wayward son.

What can we do to help face the losses we experience in our lives? For one thing, we can acknowledge the many blessings we have received: family, friends, talents, opportunities, material blessings, health. We can endeavor to appreciate them for what they are: gifts on loan. But the fact that we appreciate such gifts will not lessen the pain if we lose them. On the contrary, it might even intensify it, for often the pain of our loss is in direct proportion to the value this person or thing had in our life. At more than one wake, I have heard a grieving person say through her tears, "The problem is, I loved him too much!" Our pain of loss is often the measure of our love. It is the price we pay for love.

The price we pay for love. Recently I came across a short poem, written by a little girl, that captures beautifully what I am trying to say here:

> When my third snail died, I said,
> "I'm through with snails."
> But I didn't mean it.

Our pain of loss may make us cry out, "I'm through with loving. I'm through with life." Hopefully, with the help of Jesus, we won't mean it.

How have I experienced the pain of loss? Did anyone or anything bring me comfort or consolation during this time?

✦ Jesus, help me to see all sorrow as holy ground.

96. Jesus and Touch

Jesus then asked, "Who touched me?" —Luke 8:45

One thing that strikes me about the ministry of Jesus is how often he touched people. Already when his public ministry was in its infancy, Jesus was touching Peter's ailing mother-in-law. We read, "He approached, grasped her hand, and helped her up" (Mark 1:31). A short time later when he raised Jairus' daughter from the dead, we are told that he "took the child by the hand" (Mark 5:41). Similarly, when he expelled demons from a young boy, he reached down, grabbed the boy's hand, and helped him to stand up again (Mark 9:27).

On several occasions Jesus cured individuals by laying his hands upon them; for example, the crippled woman whom he cured on the sabbath (Luke 13:13). To the complete horror of many, Jesus touched even lepers (Mark 1:41) and prostitutes (Luke 7:38), two classes of people lumped together in the minds of many. He touched the ears of the deaf (Mark 7:33) and the eyes of the blind (Matthew 20:34). He even touched little children (Mark 10:13), much to the puzzlement of even his closest friends.

Not only did Jesus touch others, however, he also allowed others to touch him. He gave himself over to the crowds, allowing himself to be pushed and shoved as he walked along the dusty roads. He permitted individuals to grab his feet, tug at his clothing, anoint him with oil, and kiss his feet. In the end, he even gave himself over to the touch of violence, allowing himself to be scourged, mocked, beaten, and nailed to the cross.

Our Christian religion is not exactly known for being tactile. True, we have the venerable custom of the "kiss of peace," a practice we prefer to call the sign of peace. But for many, even this opportunity for sacred touch has been reduced to a limp handshake and an awkward smile. We have the sacraments, too. We have the Eucharist which we actually receive in our open hand or on our extended tongue. That's touch. In addition, we have our baptism, our anointings, our reception of ashes, our laying on of hands. I would like to think that the more we come to know the Jesus of the gospels, the more we will find creative ways to reclaim sacred touch as God's instrument of blessing and healing.

What role does touch play in my spiritual life?

✧ Jesus, touch me with your healing, and make me an instrument of healing touch for others.

97. Praying Mantras

Prayer is like a window. It is our way of opening our self to God.
—Jean Gill

Sister Kathleen Glavich, SND, a friend of mine, has written a book entitled *Prayer-Moments for Every Day of the Year.* It is a collection of hundreds of short prayers that can be used as "mantras." Kathleen explains that a mantra is a "sacred verbal formula repeated in prayer." In other words, it is a short prayer—a word, a phrase, a sentence—that is said over and over again.

Some might ask, "Why would you ever pray this way?" Kathleen gives a number of occasions when this form of prayer could prove beneficial: "when our eyes are too tired, or too weak, or too tear-filled to pray from the Bible or a prayer book." Or "when pain, physical or mental...makes us incapable of expressing a coherent thought." Or "when we are besieged...burdened...or exhausted."

The praying of a mantra can open our hearts to God's gentle prodding. It can help calm our anxiety, ease our fears, and quiet our restlessness. Mantras are wonderfully portable, that is, they can be prayed almost anywhere and anytime. Says Kathleen, "Praying a mantra is...as simple as a child incessantly crying, 'Mommy, mommy.' Yet...as meaningful and as beautiful as a lover tirelessly repeating, 'I love you.'"

The rosary is, in a way, a mantra. Over and over again we repeat the Hail Mary as our fingers move from bead to bead. I, for one, never appreciated the rosary more than when I was recovering from surgery a number of years ago. Before the surgery, I had assumed that within a day or two I would be ready to pray the psalms, as was my preference and custom. I was wrong, for when I opened my prayer book, I couldn't get my eyes to focus on the words. Frustrated, I reached for my rosary and began to pray it. Repeating those familiar words again and again gave me considerable consolation.

In her book, *Undercurrents*, Martha Manning tells that, after her grandmother's death, she was given her grandmother's rosary instead of the silver set. Says Manning: "I accept the beads from my mother, realizing that it doesn't much matter to me who gets what. My grandmother only entertained with the silver. She held on for dear life with these beads."

Do I ever pray using mantras?

✧ God, I love you...God, I love you...God, I love you.

98. Life Is a Book

The elderly are like encyclopedias: you just have to learn how to read them. —Anonymous

Conrad Bergendoof, a former college president, said in his later years: "I think of my life as a library book checked out a long time ago. The spine is cracked, the edges of the pages are frayed, and I'm long overdue. Soon the head librarian will call me in." I like that image of life as a book. It is one that theologian Martin Marty makes use of when he says, "Life is lived by chapters."

I find this image of life as a series of chapters in a book very appealing and consoling. Why? For several reasons. First, if we think of our life as one continuous essay or one long, short story, we may become unduly upset by some of the changes we encounter in life. For example, we may be asked to move far away from the place we always thought of as home. Or we may be forced to take up a new kind of work, something we have never done before. Or perhaps we experience a sudden decrease in our physical capabilities. If we assume that our life is "of a piece," we may have difficulty coping with such changes. But if, on the other hand, we think of our life as a series of chapters in a book, we might be able to face such changes with greater equanimity. Instead of thinking, "My life as I know it is ending. How awful!" we may be able to say, "Well, it looks as if this chapter in my life is drawing to a close. I wonder what the next chapter is going to be like."

The chapters in a good novel are not uniform. Some are long; some are short. Some are humorous; others are tense. Some take place in this setting; others, in that. It is this very variety that gives a novel its power and beauty. Similarly, the chapters in my life need not all be alike. They can be of different lengths, tones, and settings. By acknowledging this I can become more accepting of the many changes my life may undergo.

The Swiss philosopher Henri Frederic Amiel said, "To know how to grow old is the master-work of wisdom, and one of the most difficult chapters in the great art of life." Fortunately, however, we have many people around us who are masters of this art. These individuals have learned how to begin and end, to leave and come, to say goodbye and hello, patiently waiting for the day when the Head Librarian calls them home.

What have been some of the chapters in my own life? How good am I at beginnings and endings?

✧ God, the story of my life begins and ends with you.

99. Whose Side Are You On?

*Jesus' hour of his dying, rising, and being glorified proclaims
that God is not neutral but takes the side of the
"nonpersons" of history. —Kathleen Coyle*

Sometime during our lives we have probably said to someone,
"Whose side are you on, anyway?" Perhaps we said it to a friend who
betrayed us, or to a parent who didn't seem to understand our needs.
But if we read the Bible, we will see that this is a question frequently asked throughout salvation history: "Whose side are you on?"

It is the question Moses asked the Israelites when he came down
from the mountain and found them worshiping a golden calf. It is the
question Gideon, when he saw his country being laid waste by the
Midianites, dared to ask God. And it is the question the prophets continuously placed before their people in an effort to bring their behavior back in line with the covenant they had made with Yahweh.

Writer Jane Morrissey, SSJ, says the essential moral question is this:
"Are we on the side of virtue, or are we on the side of vice?" She
adds, "There's a turnstile open as long as we live, through which we
can pass from one side to the other."

Some of us might be uncomfortable with the notion of choosing
sides. In a culture where tolerance is almost deified, we are apt to
say, "Why talk about sides? Just let everyone believe what they want
to believe and do what they want to do—unless, of course, it's really, really wrong." Such thinking is pretty foreign to Jesus, who,
though he exemplified tolerance, nonetheless frequently talked about
taking sides, about lining up.

Remember his graphic parable of the Last Judgment? It concludes
with, "You sheep, you come here on my right. You goats, you go
over there to my left" (Matthew 25:31–46). Talk about sides! But the
truth is, we do not have to wait until the Last Judgment to see whose
side we are on, or (in terms of Jesus' parable) whether we are num-
bered with the sheep or the goats. For we can tell just by examining
the choices we are making in the here and now. We can ask ourselves: are our choices essentially selfish or altruistic? What are our
priorities? What have we taken a stand for and against lately?

The consequence of not taking sides is a severe one. Ultimately, it is death. For as Martin Luther King, Jr., has said, "We die when we refuse to stand up for what is right. We die when we refuse to take a stand for that which is true."

Whose side am I on? How can I tell?

✧ Jesus, help me to take a stand for what is right and true.

100. The Ache of Unfulfillment

In me the galaxies hunger for God. —Sebastian Moore

In the sixth book of Isaiah we read about his call from God. He tells us that this call came to him "in the year King Uzziah died" (Isaiah 6:1). That parenthetical comment roots the prophet's experience in the real world. Isaiah next describes how God appeared to him, "seated on a high and lofty throne, with the train of his garments filling the temple." The prophet did not actually see the face of God, for no human could behold God's face and live. But he did see several six-winged seraphim and heaps of smoke. He also heard the voice of God asking, "Whom shall I send? Who will go for us?" In a spontaneous burst of generosity, Isaiah says, "Here I am! Send me!" (Isaiah 6:8).

Commenting on Isaiah's vision in his book, *Cherish Christ Above All*, Demetrius Dumm, OSB, says that all believers, to a certain extent, are like Isaiah. We, too, get glimpses of God in our real world— glimpses that give our life direction and call us to ever greater love for others. Says Dumm, "God is truly present here but in an elusive way that always implies the ache of unfulfillment."

The ache of unfulfillment. In other words, we will never be completely satisfied while on earth, no matter how strong our faith, how devout our prayer, how high our morals, or how generous our love. Our glimpses of the fringes of God's robe are given not to satisfy us or to encourage us to settle down. Rather, they are given to disquiet us and to goad us to move forward. Hopefully, like St. Paul, we will eventually be able to say, "Forgetting what lies behind and straining forward to what lies ahead, I press on toward the goal, the prize of the heavenly call, in Christ Jesus" (Philippians 3:13–14).

We catch glimpses of God in this life. We strain forward. We press on. And all the while, with hope and trust and the ache of unfulfillment, we cry, "Come, Lord Jesus!" (Revelation 22:20).

How do I experience the ache of unfulfillment? How have I seen the fringes of God's robe?

✧   Come, Lord Jesus!

Bibliography

Albom, Mitch. *Tuesdays with Morrie*. New York: Doubleday, 1997.

Bennett, William. *The Book of Virtues*. New York: Simon and Schuster, 1993.

Bly, Richard, ed. *Times Alone: Selected Poems of Antonio Machado*. Middletown, CT: University Press of New England, 1983.

Buber, Martin. *Between Man and Man*. New York: Macmillan, 1985.

DeMello, Anthony. *Wellsprings: A Book of Spiritual Exercises*. New York: Doubleday, 1985.

Dillard, Annie. *Pilgrim at Tinker Creek*. New York: Bantam Books, 1974.

Dumm, Demetrius, OSB. *Cherish Christ above All*. Mahwah, NJ: Paulist Press, 1996.

Glavich, Kathleen, SND. *Prayer Moments for Every Day of the Year*. Mystic, CT: Twenty-Third Publications, 1998.

Gorsuch, John P. *An Invitation to the Spiritual Journey*. Mahwah, NJ: Paulist Press, 1990.

Haughton, Rosemary. *The Catholic Thing*. Springfield, IL: Templegate, 1979.

Hillesum, Etty. *An Interrupted Life*. New York: Pantheon Books, 1983.

Lamott, Anne. *Bird by Bird*. New York: Doubleday, 1994.

L'Engle, Madeleine. *Walking on Water*. Wheaton, IL: Harold Shaw Publishers, 1980.

Lewis, C.S. *The Screwtape Letters*. New York: Macmillan, 1982.

Manning, Martha. *Undercurrents: A Life Beneath the Surface*. New York: HarperCollins, 1995.

Merton, Thomas. *Seeds of Contemplation*. New York: New Directions Press, 1949.

Moore, Sebastian. *The Inner Loneliness*. New York: Crossroad, 1984.

Morneau, Robert. *Fathoming Bethlehem: Advent Meditations*. New York: Crossroad, 1997.

Norris, Kathleen. *Amazing Grace*. New York: Penguin Putnam, 1998.

Pollard, Miriam, OSCO. *The Listening God*. Collegeville, MN: Michael Glazier, 1989.

Rupp, Joyce, OSM. *Dear Heart, Come Home*. New York: Crossword, 1997.

Shea, John. *The God Who Fell from Heaven*. Allen, TX: Thomas More Press, 1992.

Senior, Donald, CP. *Jesus: A Gospel Portrait*. Dayton: Pflaum Books, 1975.

Weil, Simone. *Waiting on God*. London: Routledge and Kegan, 1952.

Index

The number cited refers to the number of the meditation.

adversity - 10, 17, 25, 51, 54, 62, 78, 84
aging - 30, 71, 78, 84, 98
ambiguity - 88
ancestors - 86
Angelus - 39
animals - 15, 19, 41, 72, 90
Annunciation - 32
art - 63
attention - 41, 46, 89
attitude - 40, 48, 56

beauty - 11, 31, 39
beginnings - 34, 98

change - 37, 55, 71, 98
children - 53, 60, 65
commitment - 99
community - 16, 23, 51, 58, 74
compassion (see also love) - 27, 40
conversion - 94
countercultural - 21
creativity - 81
criticism - 18
cynicism - 24

dance - 44
darkness - 17
death - 13, 30, 95
decisions - 34, 42, 66
desire - 28, 92
detachment - 20, 37
devil - 38

direction - 33, 66
discernment - 34
discipleship - 20, 45, 58, 75
doubt - 88

ecology - 15, 41, 49
ego - 69
endings - 34, 98
Eucharist - 86
evil - 38
example - 67
excellence - 94

faith - 10, 21, 23, 29, 50, 74, 76, 78, 81, 82, 86, 88
family - 25, 86
fear - 1, 63
forgiveness - 3, 4
freedom - 21
friendship - 58
fulfillment - 100

garden - 43
generativity - 9
God - 28, 47, 60, 63, 85, 100
goodness - 5, 22
giving - 32
golden rule - 77
gratitude - 11, 25, 89
growth - 55

habit - 22
heaven - 13
help - 90

holiness - 5
honesty - 19
hope - 24
humility - 57
humor - 14, 65, 53, 87, 93

imagination - 81
Incarnation - 39

Jesus - 35, 66, 68, 70, 75, 80, 96
judgment - 26
justice - 92, 99

kingdom of God - 16

Last Judgment - 99
laughter - 14, 87
Lent - 29
letting go - 37
liturgy - 23, 88
loss - 95
love - 3, 4, 8, 12, 27, 28, 40, 43,
      44, 50, 51, 57, 58, 67, 73, 76,
      77, 79, 83, 85, 91, 95

manners - 77
mantras - 97
Mary - 32
Mass (see liturgy)
mourning - 68, 95

nature - 15, 31, 41, 43, 62, 72,
      89
needs - 90

optimism - 91
ordinary - 6

patience - 17, 52
peace - 79
penance - 57, 64, 73
perseverance - 78, 84
petition - 90
plants - 43, 62
prayer - 1, 12, 33, 39, 59, 60, 61,
      90, 91, 92, 97
prepositions - 16
proverbs - 36, 65, 93
psalms - 61

receiving - 32
religion - 50
repentance - 94
renunciation - 20
respect 40
responsibility - 1
restlessness - 100
reverence - 49
role models - 84
romance - 8
rosary - 97
routine - 12

St. Joseph - 10
St. Peter - 19
saints - 5
seeking - 92
self-esteem - 7, 27, 69, 91
self-knowledge - 18, 26
sensitivity - 67
serenity - 54
service - 67
sin - 26, 60
sleep - 46
sorrow - 95
spiritual health - 2

spirituality - 46
stewardship - 15
stories - 82
stress - 33, 59
suffering - 25
surprise - 71, 72

thanksgiving (see also
    gratitude) - 25
time - 33, 52, 59, 89
touch - 96
trust - 52, 53
truth - 11

unfulfillment - 100
unity - 23

violence - 79
virtue - 22
vulnerability - 68, 69

wakefulness - 46
weakness - 68
words - 70
work - 64, 76, 83
writing - 35

Also by Melannie Svoboda

Abundant Treasures
Meditations on the Many Gifts of the Spirit

The Spirit rushes into even the smallest and seemingly least significant corners of our lives with gifts that can transform us. These gifts, 51 to be exact, include quotations, meditations, prayers, and reflection questions to help readers focus on and appreciate the abundant riches present in their lives.   999-8, 128 pp, $9.95

Teaching is Like…
Peeling Back Eggshells

Warm and witty, these fifty reflections will sustain enthusiasm, bolster morale, and encourage teaching as a gracefilled privilege.   613-1, 120 pp, $7.95

Jesus, I'm a Teacher, Too
Guidance and Inspiration from the Gospels

Great for personal or group prayer, this book focuses on Jesus' teaching ministry in the Gospel of St. Mark as a model for teachers and catechists.
          645-X, 144 pp, $9.95

Everyday Epiphanies
Seeing the Sacred in Every Thing

These 175 short reflections are divided according to the seasons of the year, and each ends with a reflection prayer. Topics range from the mundane to the unusual and unexpected and each reflection invites readers to discover God in every aspect of our lives. Scripture passages scattered throughout offer insights into the ways that Jesus used the occurrences of everyday living to reveal both God and grace.   730-8, 192 pp, $9.95

Traits of a Healthy Spirituality

Here Sr. Melannie describes twenty indicators of a healthy spirituality, including: self-esteem, friendship, courage, tolerance, joy, and forgiveness. She demonstrates how to use these signs to determine where we stand in terms of our Christian spirituality. Includes meditations, questions for reflection, and closing prayers.
          698-0, 144 pp, $9.95